Advance Praise and Recommendations for
THE FRUGAL BOOK PROMOTER

At last—a solid, sensible, systematic guide to the ins and outs of promotion and publicity. Written by a writer, *for* writers—Carolyn Howard-Johnson proves that she's not only an accomplished poet, essayist, and novelist, but also a marketing maestro!
> JayCe Crawford, CUP OF COMFORT author, music copyright professional

The whole promotion or lack of promotion from publishers is something that I find confusing. They print, distribute, ship and then let the majority of their books just die! It's a nutty business model. Hence I'm very interested in your e-book!
> Eric Dinyer, author/photographer of EFFORT AND SURRENDER

(Carolyn Howard-Johnson is) an incessant promoter who develops and shares new approaches for book promotion.
> Marilyn Ross, Founder of Small Publishers of North America and author of THE COMPLETE GUIDE TO SELF PUBLISHING

THE FRUGAL BOOK PROMOTER. I love it. Most authors don't have "deep pockets" for publicity, promotion and marketing; this is the kind of information *we* need! The chapter on the perks available on Amazon is a perfect example of the kind of practical advice offered—the kind that took me months to discover.
> Rolf Gompertz, author, veteran publicist for NBC and UCLA instructor.

The Frugal Book Promoter offers practical advice the author has gleaned from personal experience. Unlike other books and articles on the subject, this one is detailed—and it's chock full of ideas that even seasoned book promoters will not have tried.
> Dallas Hodder Franklin, author and editor of www.SellWritingOnline.com

Wow. What more can I say? Interesting, informative, readable and more. Easy to follow, quotes and technique mixed in together wonderfully. This is an A-one job. Watch out world! I'm going to have to put it under my pillow.
> Leora G. Krygier, author of FIRST THE RAVEN and WHEN SHE SLEEPS

The Frugal Book Promoter:
How To Do What Your Publisher Won't

or

Nitty-Gritty How-Tos for Getting Nearly Free
Publicity

The Frugal Book Promoter:
How To Do What Your Publisher Won't

or

Nitty-Gritty How-Tos for Getting Nearly Free
Publicity

By Carolyn Howard-Johnson

THE FRUGAL BOOK PROMOTER

ISBN: 1-932993-10-X (trade paperback)
1-932993-11-8 (e-book version)

Library of Congress Number
LCCN: 2004095529

Edited by T.C. McMullen
Cover and Interior Design by
Mystique Design and Editorial

Published in 2004 by Star Publish

Printed in the United States of America

A Star Publish Book
http://starpublish.com
Nevada, U.S.A. and St. Croix, U.S.V.I.

The

a.1. A word placed before nouns to limit or individualize their meaning.

Fru´gal

a. 1. Economical in the use or appropriation of resources; not wasteful or lavish; wise in the expenditure or application of force, materials, time, etc.; characterized by frugality; sparing; economical; saving; as, a frugal housekeeper; frugal of time.

Book

n. 1. A collection of sheets of paper, or similar material, blank, written, or printed, bound together; commonly, many folded and bound sheets containing continuous printing or writing.
2. A composition, written or printed; a treatise.

Pro-mot´er

n. 1. One who, or that which, forwards, advances, or promotes; an encourager; as, a promoter of charity or philosophy.
2. Specifically, one who sets on foot, and takes the preliminary steps in, a scheme for the organization of a corporation, a joint-stock company, or the like.

Dedication

This book is dedicated to Mary Pappasideris Chachas, my first demanding editor, and the late Eleanor Lambert of the Eleanor Lambert Agency, New York, who showed me that publicity is a matter of style. It is also dedicated to you, the author-publicist of the new millennium.

In Memoriam to Hazel McElroy Cutler
1923 – 2004
whose chosen career centered on books and libraries.

Acknowledgements

...traditional marketers count dollars; guerrilla marketers count relationships.

Jay Conrad Levinson, THE GUERILLA MARKETING series.

Oh, to remember all those who have been instrumental in the birth of a book! Once, at a writers' seminar, I overheard a well-known author deride writers who listed many as their mentors and helpmates as a ridiculous name-dropping tradition. He is a wonderful writer but I feel that he must have an inflated opinion of his own abilities if he believes he writes his books by himself. He may also be a very poor publicist for the nourishing elements of PR are offering to help others, accepting help from others and being grateful for the growth that comes from that exchange. My thank you list is long, but probably not nearly long enough. My apologies to those who have contributed and been— momentarily—forgotten.

Thanks to Millie Szerman, author of VIEW FROM THE TUB (www.stairwellpress.com), whose nudges I sometimes ignore, but whose encouragement is always appreciated.

Thanks to JayCe Crawford, (www.authorsden.com/jaycecrawford), author of "The Road," a well-known short story about love and loss that has been used by the youth division of the California Superior Court to help rehabilitate young speed offenders and Leora G. Krygier, (www.authorsden.com/leorgkrygier), author of two sensitive literary novels, FIRST THE RAVEN and WHEN SHE SLEEPS. They are my critique partners and kindred hearts whose successes and problems with marketing or the lack of it helped inspire this book. And to my own Chevy Chase Library Critique Group for the same reasons. They manage to give me much more than I give.

To publicist Debra Gold, for general, loving support and a way with words that inspires me to do better and to Rolf Gompertz, (www.authorsden.com/rolfgompertz), author of ABRAHAM THE DREAMER, whose public relations expertise is always insightful.

Thank you to my publisher, Margie Tovrea, who encouraged me to publish this book as a paperback and e-book, a double whammy, rather than only as an e-book as I had originally planned. Thank you, too, to Margie's talented associate, T.C. McMullen, cover artist, editor, formatter. That both are authors in their own right gives them an understanding of how particular an author can be about presenting her book—her obsession—in the right light. And, thank you to all those who cheerfully gave me permission to quote them and to relate their PR successes and disasters.

And last but not least, to my husband Lance Johnson who was not too busy to apply his organized and unrelenting passion for detail to editing THE FRUGAL BOOK PROMOTER: HOW TO DO WHAT YOUR PUBLISHER WON'T when he was in the throes of polishing his own book WHAT ASIANS SHOULD KNOW ABOUT AMERICA, FROM A TO Z, soon to be published in China in translation.

If I had tried for years to get an agent and get published, then maybe I would feel differently...but for me, the scary part is about to start right now.

Lara Vapnyar, author of THERE ARE JEWS IN MY HOUSE when she learned she must publicize her first book

Foreword

In terms of promotion it matters not a whit who publishes your book, *you,* dear author, must learn to promote it if you want to give it a fighting chance on the freeways of commerce. If your name isn't King, Grafton, Oates or Bradbury, forget a free ride. Even famous names like these once paid their promotion dues and some still are. John Grisham's story about selling books—store to store, person to person, out of the trunk of his car—is legend, if not letter-perfect true.

Further—and this is the more vital part of this message—no matter how big the budget or adept the publicity and advertising department of your publisher, there are some things they cannot do as well as you can. They, after all, are the publishers. For the public, the magic is in the author's name, her smile, her story, her signature.

Introduction

It is said that business and art don't mix. Actually they mix very well. The chances of success for artists who are natural promoters (Think Warhol. Think Dickens.) grow incrementally compared to artists who prefer to remain cloistered.

The reasons that authors tend to fail at promotion are two-fold. They think they must only show up at bookstores with a good pen because that's all that is expected of Hilary Clinton or J.K. Rowling. They may be frightened by the magnitude of what they suspect they must do to give birth to this book of theirs—their baby—and so they dig in their heels and go into a severe state of denial.

This book addresses both groups. That you, the author—experienced or just blooming—hold this how-to book in your hands means that you *know* you need to hone your marketing skills in order to put this child of yours on the path to success. This book will, indeed, help you plan a campaign suitable for the realities of the publishing world.

THE FRUGAL BOOK PROMOTER will lead you up the publicity rungs of the publishing ladder. You'll learn what you might do before your book is published, what you must do soon after it is published and beyond. Consider everything offered, as if you were testing desserts at a smorgasbord; then select what suits your book, your personality and your pocketbook.

This book is designed so that authors who already have experience with publicity can select chapters that address aspects of their marketing plan that are weak. If a reference is made to something covered in more depth elsewhere, the reader is given a prompt.

Hint: Do not skip the chapters on mailing lists even if you already have one. An effective campaign is only as sound as this essential database and the hints therein are the product of more than three decades of publicity experience in the fashion, retailing and publishing industries.

Most ideas are presented in practical, easy steps; you'll also find hints and caveats indented for easy review.

When you finish this book you'll know what it took me—with a publicity background—three years to learn. Publicity for authors is a specialized arena of public relations. I tripped and fell into many PR potholes; negative experiences can be good teachers but learning from a book like this is less painful.

THE FRUGAL BOOK PROMOTER is not a text. It contains many opinions—some as black and white as the page you find them on. You may also notice omissions. I avoided topics that have been covered ad infinitum and for which I have nothing new to add but you will find some new (or rarely used) ways to promote that have not been scorched, stirred and then warmed over.

Table of Contents

A PR Primer

One Dozen Publicity No-Nos

or

How to Avoid Being a PR Numbskull

(This is an example of a "tip sheet." You'll learn more about tips sheets and how to use them later in this book.)

1. Don't assume your publisher will publicize for you.
2. Don't publicize your book; instead "brand" yourself.
3. Don't ask an editor, producer or host for "publicity." They are not in business to do favors for you.
4. Don't send a publicity or a news release. It's a "media release."
5. Don't send material to media professionals who have been dead for over a year or were fired for showing preferential treatment to friends.
6. Don't avoid all controversy. It may be your prescription for getting noticed.
7. Don't discard the word "ethics" from your campaign.
8. Don't pretend those who visit your website are only there to purchase your book.
9. Don't depend only on e-mails and faxes to get the word out to editors and booksellers.
10. Don't toss your books on marketing into your circular file once your book has been launched.
11. Don't treat your book sales like a hobby.
12. Don't believe everything about publicizing books (or writing them!) that you read on the Web. Consider the source. Check credentials.

> Hint: In this book you will find more on each no-no, accompanied by a recommendation for how to correct each faux pas. When you are done, you'll be able to identify publicity curbs you might trip over and have new publicity tools to maneuver through the book marketing maze.

Section I

It's Never Too Early to Think About Marketing

Promotion is a not a sprint but a marathon. As any coach knows, you start training slowly and build up steam.

CHJ, from the Palm Springs Writers' Guild Newsletter

The aim of marketing is to make selling superfluous. The aim is to know and understand the customer so well that the product or service fits him and sells itself.

Peter Drucker, management theorist

Chapter 1: Addressing Numbing Fears

Having our voice heard is more important than selling books. Having our voice heard is sharing our soul.
CHJ, from MyShelf.com Back to Literature column

Have you heard other authors express these doubts? "If I publish my work will someone steal it?" "If I market it are the chances for being ripped off increased?" "I'm a writer, not a speaker or actor or publicist and I'm scared." Do you feel that way yourself?

Publishing is a great adventure. Because so much of a great publicity campaign involves *exposing* your writing (press releases, columns, reviews and more), it is important that those about to publish come to terms with some of the fears that will keep them grounded when they should be flying high.

Fear of Plagiarism

You have a memory that would convict any author of plagiarism in any court of literature in the world.
John Hawkesworth of Samuel Johnson

The fear of plagiarism can surely paralyze a writer if it isn't addressed.

Among the writers I meet on the Web, in my critique groups, in my classes—wherever authors get together—plagiarism is sure to eventually be a topic of discussion. Some writers are crippled by the fear that someone will steal their idea. It keeps many from sending their work to publishers and agents, deters others from seeking spotlights that will assure the success of their books.

29

The most important part of writing after the process itself is to be read, to *share*. All this worry about plagiarism keeps inexperienced writers from doing that. Not only that, it may produce anxieties that interfere with their creativity.

Excepting for spurring an author to take precautions, worrying about plagiarism, copyright, and "giving away an idea" instead of about sharing talent, is destructive. I would rather have a million people read one of my poems credited only as "Anonymous" in a Dear Abby column than have it read not at all. I fervently hope more writers will come to share this view.

The kind of plagiarism that authors worry about is quite rare. Often cases are reported but when the perpetrator is found innocent, the case has lost its news value. Certainly, when it occurs among those who have the public trust, it gets lots of press. Careers of a few writers have been broken into kindling when plagiarism was uncovered; sometimes however, the opposite happens. Near-anonymous writers or those relegated to the obscure halls of academia become household names when they are found to have picked clean the bones of others' words. Recently names like Stephen Ambrose and Doris Kearns Goodwin became known among people who would never have heard of them before.

It is also true that much plagiarism takes place that never sees the light of day because the thief is not caught or his work is so poor that even stealing cannot make it star-worthy. But think! Think! How much is written, published, put out into the world. The chance that your work might get stolen is minuscule.

Plagiarism is most rampant in academia. If you need proof, do a Google.com search on plagiarism. Yep, a few famous cases and lots of kids trying to make the grade at school. We cannot condone such theft but we authors should not allow it to doom our work to perdition, only the poor young schmuck who grabbed down someone else's work will suffer—whether or not he is caught.

Another consideration: If someone should swipe a few of your words or an idea, his chances of becoming rich, famous and envied because of them are no better than yours. If he should, that sets him up for a legal suit worth pursuing. If he doesn't get rich on your work, you have the satisfaction of knowing he didn't and won't need to bother your talented head about chasing after a pauper. You might even benefit; the publicity that might surround such a case could be the lucky stroke that makes *you* a rich, famous, and envied author. Publicity is what makes a book a commodity. Sometimes the worst possible scenario you can imagine can be a blessing. Ask any excellent public relations professional; she'll show you how to make a sweet drink out of very sour fruit.

I've written and published hundreds of articles and reviews in the last couple years and not one—to my knowledge—has been plagiarized. None of my students have had their material "borrowed," either. This means that my poetry, short stories, excerpts, flash fiction and even quotes are seeing the light of day. Can't knock that!

Consider, also, that there is no truly original idea in the world, so even your most creative inspiration will certainly have been used by someone else in the past. Joseph Campbell published a raft of books that examines this subject for the benefit of all students of literature.

Ask yourself what is the worst thing that can happen. Convince yourself that it is worse to allow yourself to be paralyzed by something that may never come to pass.

In the meantime, here are ways you can protect yourself.
1. Copyright large works with the copyright office for $30. Go to www.copyright.gov for instructions.
2. Copyright both your longer and shorter pieces by sending yourself a copy in a sealed envelope. Mark it "Copyright" plus the title of your piece. Don't disturb the seal when it arrives. File it. This untouched envelope and contents is acceptable "proof" the material is yours.
3. Once your work is published, take a few minutes every 90 days or so, to self-surf the Web. Type a phrase from one of your pieces into the search engine with quotes around it. If those exact words have been used, you will find them. You'll probably find that these words aren't attached to the rest of any work that belongs to you but the process will reassure you.

You might also bolster your confidence by trying this exercise: Ask three writers (critique group friends, perhaps) to write a piece using a very specific subject—maybe even something you've considered writing yourself. I did this with a friend's idea after asking permission to use it. It was a story about how, as a child, she sneaked into a neighbor's house and ate frosted strawberries out of the Fridge. We then set a lunch date and read each work aloud. They were so different we wondered why we had been concerned about a fellow writer stealing an idea. Usually, a writer won't be interested in writing someone else's "stuff," anyway. Writing, after all is about *self* expression.

> Caveat #1: Ideas are easier to steal than finished works, nonfiction easier than fiction.

> Caveat #2: It is as important that you guard against inadvertently plagiarizing someone else's material as that you protect your own. If you research material for your writing, take every precaution against it.

Fear of Success or Rejection

> *Go on, my friend, and fear nothing; you carry Cæsar and his fortunes in your boat.*
> Plutarch, from "Life of Ceasar"

Psychology journals are full of information about the fear of success or rejection. Some little voice nags you that you won't be successful when really there is something inside your head screaming, "And what if you are?" or the other way around. A good therapist can help you with this. A book for writers that addresses several of the psychological intricacies of writing is Bruce Holland Rogers' WORD WORKS, available on Amazon. If you even suspect— remotely—that either of these might be your problem check one or both. In the meantime, I suggest taking baby steps to overcome them.

Here a few steps that may get you toddling. They work better when you say them out loud:
- Today I am going to dig up one old piece I wrote from the bowels of my computer.
- Today I am going to rewrite or edit it.
- Today I am going to buy the newest edition of WRITER'S MARKETS published by Writer's Digest Books.
- Today I am going to find one magazine, journal or publisher in WRITER'S MARKETS that might be interested in that work.

- Today I am going to address the envelope and maybe even (gasp! *Two* baby steps?) write the cover letter that goes with it. (WRITER'S MARKETS has samples of both query and cover letters).
- Today I am going to put my cover letter and written work into the envelope and stamp it.
- Today I am going to mail it.

When all these tiny efforts have been made, your first giant step has been taken. Add love, a pat on the back and repeat. Do this at least 13 times in succession; those balls in the air help mask your fears.

How does this writing and publishing help you promote your book? It's all about something called branding (see chapter two). Every time your byline appears, you are making editors, agents, webmasters, and other writers aware of you and what you do. Every time you are published, for pay or not, your tagline (see chapter two) appears complete with a link to your website, your e-mail address or a bookseller's site. Every time you are published, that achievement becomes part of your résumé, part of your media kit, part of the confidence you need to promote with your chin up and a brave smile on your face.

You want to submit the most professional proposal, synopsis and chapters that you can because the image you create—from the very beginning—is part of your overall promotion plan. This is my list of possibilities in order of my preference:

- Take classes from a reputable college that specializes in classes for writers in both writing and the business of publishing. I used UCLA's Writers' Program and now teach there. Contact mhenness@unex.ucla.edu to receive their Writers' Quarterly. It is an entertaining journal for writers and lists the school's online and traditional classes.
- Join a critique group or assemble a group from members of classes you have taken. The latter is better because you'll know these members have a background in writing and the critique process.
- Purchase books on editing, grammar, the elements of writing, marketing and more. Many are recommended within these pages.
- Utilize experienced support people:
  - M. Rachel Plummer can teach you how to structure

a professionally written manuscript. Go to: http://www.how2writeabook.com/indexff.htm

- Eve Lasalle Caram teaches and critiques privately. Reach her at ecaram1@earthlink.net.

- Use the Web as a resource for individual needs. Black on White is a website designed to help writers overcome hurdles including fear: http://www.blackonwhite.on.ca/welcome.html

Chapter 2: Learn to Play the PR Game

Public relations is neither advertising nor free ink.
It is the dissemination of information that sets a
standard for how you would like to be perceived.
First and foremost, it must be undertaken with the
highest ethical standards.

CHJ, from Home Décor Buyer, Inside Retailing
column

This chapter—this book, in fact—cannot teach you everything you
should know about public relations. We're playing pick up sticks
here and I'm tossing out some aspects of public relations that you
will need to promote your book and to brand your author-self.
What I offer may be all you *need* to know, but I urge you to learn
more anyway. You will find sources in this chapter and others that
will nurture your understanding of the broader world of marketing
and public relations; if you already have a background in these
subjects, dig out your old texts and review them.

I encourage authors to start on their publicity campaign early. Your
book may not even be done. You may not have an agent or a
publisher. Here is why it is best—no matter where you are in the
publishing process—to start now:

- To be effective, publicity must build.
- You can't possibly learn all you need to know in one
  evening. Best to start now.
- Publicity is like practicing piano. The more you do it, the
  better it will play in Peoria and everywhere else.
- What you know about publicity early on and the exposure
  you receive now will work in your favor when you go after
  an agent or publisher.

These pick up sticks I'm lobbing at you come in all colors. There
are the kinds that cost you nothing out-of-pocket and those that

cost more. They will all cost you some time. Some are essential if you want to succeed at the game, others are nice additions.

Even if you choose to hire someone to do most of your publicity for you, expect that you will need to carve time from your schedule and extra dollars from your budget. You'll also need to learn something about the process in order to work as a team with whomever you hire or with—and heaven has truly blessed you if you should have access to this—a publicist who has been assigned to you by your publisher.

Publicity is not a quantifiable science. It is difficult if not impossible to trace a direct line from your promotional efforts to the sale of a book. If an author measures the success of her efforts toward getting publicity for her book by the number she sells or the column inches she gets in ink, she may very well consider herself unsuccessful unless she hits it big and snags an interview on "Today." On the other hand, if she thinks of her efforts as a process—toward branding, or long-term image making—her efforts will eventually be rewarded in significant ways.

Too often an author elects to write her book and then sits back and never turns a hand to market it—not before her book comes out, not at its release, not after. Here is what might happen to an author who tries to dodge a promotional campaign:
- Unless the universe is truly smiling on her she will neither sell many books, nor will her publisher be endeared to her.
- Her book—perhaps years of work—will be out of print in very short order. She'll see it again, trashed on the remainder pile in discount book stores.
- If she self or subsidy publishes, the book will be available but it will languish.
- Even if her writing is stellar, an author whose sales record is dismal or one who has no marketing skills may have trouble retaining or finding an agent for her next book.

Here are some essentials about promotion, publicity and public relations. More will come later.

What is PR, Anyway?
>Without publicity there can be no public support...
>Benjamin Disraeli

The founder of a huge retail chain once said that advertising works, we just don't know how, why, or where it works best.

What we do know is that advertising's less mysterious cousin, publicity, works even better. It is the more reliable relative because it is judged on its merit alone and carries the cachet of an editor's approval. It also is surrounded by the ever-magic word "free." The two are easily identified as kin along with promotion and public relations.

Advertising and publicity often walk hand-in-hand, yet they can be incompatible. The editors of good media outlets will not allow their advertising department to influence their editorial staff. Still, in an effort to be impartial, they reserve the right to use advertisers' stories editorially if they deem them newsworthy. That is why it is helpful (but certainly not necessary) to advertise. If you do, choose a vehicle that plays to the audience you would like to see standing in line for your book. This paid-for exposure then becomes an entrée to the editorial (another word for all that space or exposure that isn't paid-for advertising) decision-makers. Your contact in the advertising department may be willing to put your media release on the desk of his editors to look at. He should not promise you results, but his efforts may help. If you try this route, choose a "little pond," a local weekly or an arty quarterly; that way the dollars you spend will be noticed.

Sometimes a magazine or newspaper will run a special promotion called advertorial. These are sections where you pay for an ad and a reporter is assigned to cover the story you want told. This article may be "free" with the purchase of an ad or you may actually purchase the advertorial, usually at a cheaper price than a display ad of the same size would cost. This advertorial carries some of the prestige of editorial copy—that is the general reader may assume the article has been chosen only on its merits because of its copycat character. The writer or editor you meet can be more effectively approached when you have something exceptional you want to submit as honest-to-goodness news.

Advertorial isn't exactly FREE and display advertising certainly isn't! If FREE sounds more like the fare that will serve your needs, carve out some time to do it yourself and follow these commandments:

19 Commandments for Getting Free Publicity

Here is a short public relations course: Good PR is carefully targeted. It is PR in which the recipient feels cared for, PR that is repeated—with love and expertise—over and over again. Those are the essentials and they work

CHJ, from the National Association of Women Writers' newsletter.

1. Educate yourself:

- Study other's media releases and edit them according to the guidelines in WRITING EFFECTIVE NEWS RELEASES by Catherine V. McIntyre. It is available at Amazon.com.
- Read PUBLICITY ADVICE & HOW-TO HANDBOOK by UCLA Extension's Marketing Instructor, Rolf Gompertz. Order it by calling (818) 980-3576.
- Subscribe to writing-oriented e-letters like Krista Barrett's at http://www.writergazette.
- Join organizations of like-minded authors; subscribe to their newsletters. One of the best is SPAN CONNECTION put out by the Small Publishers of North America, www.spannet.org.
- Lots of free publicity can be found on the net. Learn more about it with COMPLETE GUIDE TO INTERNET PUBLICITY by Steve O'Keefe http://www.patronsaintpr.com, or INTERNET MARKETING FOR DUMMIES by Frank Catalano & Bud Smith.
- Check out THE GUERILLA MARKETING series by Jay Conrad Levinson from Houghton Mifflin.
- For marketing basics, everyone loves FREE PRIZE INSIDE by Seth Godin.

2. Read, read, read: *notice opportunity*

My daughter found a flier from the local library in the Sunday paper stuffed between grocery coupons. It mentioned a display done by a local merchant in the library window. I have that on my to-do list. Your newspaper, your e-zines, your rubbish (and that includes SPAM) can be the goose that laid the golden egg.

3. Keep an open mind for promotion ideas:

Look at the different themes in your book to find angles you can exploit when you're talking to editors. E-books are big news right now. Poetry books are selling better now than ever before. A romance website would like my book, THIS IS THE PLACE, but so would a literary one. That it is set in Salt Lake City, the site where the winter games were played in 2002 was an unexpected publicity bonus. I found sports desks and feature editors open to it as Olympics fervor grew and even as it waned because they still needed news and had used all the closely related material they had access to.

4. Cull contacts:

Add media contacts to your Rolodex. The website http://www.gebbieinc.com/ has an All-in-One Directory that links others. Some partial directories on the Web are free and so are your yellow pages. Ask for help from your librarian — a good research librarian is like a shark; she'll keep biting until she's got exactly what she wants. *(Maryjo)*

5. Etiquette counts:

Send thank-you notes to contacts after they've featured you or your book. This happens so rarely they are sure to be impressed and to pay attention to the next idea you have, even if it's just a listing in a calendar for your next book signing.

6. Partner with your publicist and publisher:

Ask for help from their promotion departments — even if it's just for a sample media release, or a .jpeg of your book cover. Give them a good reason to feature your book more prominently on their website.

7. Publicize who you are, what you do:

Reviews aren't the only way to find readers. Utilize the fame you may have accrued in your day job. Several editors have liked the idea that I wrote my first book at an age when most are thinking of retiring; they see me as an example that it is never too late to follow a dream.

8. Develop new activities to publicize:

Don't do what every other author does.
- Utah author Marilyn Brown, author of GHOSTS OF THE OQUIRRHS, gives an annual writers' award in her name. Some colleges and writers' organizations encourage scholarships. Community service makes you feel good and you'll receive coverage when you announce it, when you

name judges, when you submit names and pictures of the contestants and when you hold a gala to honor winners.

- Use your imagination for a spectacular launch. Involve a local dignitary. Get charities involved.
- Throw a party for reasons other than a book launch—a salon perhaps where artists of all kinds pool their lists to provide a spectacular and varied day for their friends and for the press.
- Offer to speak to groups and organizations.

throughout midweek on initiation

9. Don't overlook your day-to-day book-related news:

You may not even recognize what seems mundane to you as news. What is important is how the press views them. You can even manufacture reasons to send out a release. Here are five things your local newspaper may want to know about:

- You are asked to teach at your local college.
- A publisher asks you to act as an advisor or ombudsman.Mine did and I didn't think of it as an occasion for a release until later.
- You participate on a book fair panel on writing.
- A nationally known journal publishes an excerpt from your book.

10. Your readers:

Listen to your readers. You'll find a human interest angle that will make you a hero to a columnist and your book may get mentioned in the story she writes.

11. Your personal life:

Your local newspaper might regularly publish pictures of residents holding the front page as they stand proudly before some foreign monument during their travels to China or Battle Creek. Your son gets engaged, married, has a baby. You're elected secretary of Kiwanis. You hit a hole in one. Some media don't use these kinds of things but some TV stations and small papers sure do and the fact that you are also a published author makes you more newsworthy. Don't forget to use your short bio when you send them the news: "Ms. P.R. Brilliant is the author of three novels and sits on the board of the Sioux City Public Library."

12. Calamities:

Do a good turn during a crisis. Donate books for earthquake victims to read while they are waiting for permanent shelters.

13. Send professional photos with your release:

Request guidelines from your target media. Local editors won't mind if you send a homey Kodak moment—properly labeled—along with your release. Some will use what you send; your snaps may pique the interest of others and they'll ask to send out their own photographers. It's best, however, to send only professional photos to the big guys.

14. Frequency is important: *Persistence*

The editor who ignores your first release may pay more attention to your second or twenty-fifth. She will come to view you as a source and call you when she needs to quote an expert. Novelists qualify as well as writers of nonfiction. I received a nice referral in my local newspaper because I am now an "expert" on prejudice, even though my book is a novel and not a how-to or self-help piece.

> Hint: Authors of books other than your own need experts, too. Find those who might still be working on books in your subject area at your library's research desk in FORTHCOMING BOOKS IN PRINT. Send each a letter, introduce yourself and offer specific suggestions on how the information you have might be used in their book.

15. Follow up:

Shel Horowitz, author of MARKETING WITHOUT MEGABUCKS at http://www.frugalfun.com, reports that follow-up calls boost the chances of a press release being published. Voice contact builds relationships better than other means of communication.

16. Keep clippings:

Professional publicists like Debra Gold of Gold & Company do this for their clients; you do it so you'll know what's working and what isn't.

17. Evaluate:

One year after your first release, add up your column inches. Measure the number of free inches any paper gave you including headlines and pictures. If the piece is three columns wide and each column of your story is six inches long, that is 18 column inches.

How much does that newspaper charge per inch for their ads? Multiply the column inches by that rate to know what the piece is worth in advertising dollars. Now add 20 percent for the additional trust the reader puts in editorial material.

18. Set goals:

You now have a total of what your year's efforts have reaped. New publicist-authors should set a goal to increase that amount by 100 percent in the next year. If you already have a track record, aim for 20 percent.

19. Observe progress:

Publicity is like planting bulbs. It proliferates even when you aren't trying very hard. By watching for unintended results, you learn how to make them happen in the future.

Free Publicity Isn't Free

> If I had to pay me, I couldnt afford my services.
> Rolf Gompertz, author and UCLA Extension's 30 year veteran marketing instructor.

This quote is not only a poignant reminder of how important it is for an author to know something about promotion but it dispels the notion that getting publicity requires little money or time. Rolf Gompertz, author of ABRAHAM THE DREAMER, has managed the publicity on behalf of his own books. Gompertz (rolfgompertz@yahoo.com) is a good friend, a good publicist and he makes me laugh.

I don't want to lead you astray. "Free" publicity costs, whether you hire a publicist or do it yourself. Stamps, envelopes, paper, ink cartridges, and maybe even a new computer must be paid for. Throw tons of learning and execution time into the mix. I asked Gompertz, who also has 30 years experience doing publicity for NBC, to give me an accounting of the runs he made to Office Depot for book promotion materials:

> "Sending out copies of your book costs money, but it can pay off if you get a good review, print article or broadcast interview out of it. (Those books) you send out aren't free. No matter how you publish, you need to project the cost of sample books into your budget. I probably sent out 50 books for a total of $523.25. Dan Poynter, one of the most successful self-

publishers, suggests that sending out 600 books is one of the cheapest ways of getting publicity.

(Because he is self-published his unit book price is low so 600 books would have cost him $1200). Some traditionally published authors are able to negotiate a certain number of copies with their publishers, but only a very few send out many books for their midlist authors.

"Even my do-it-yourself media kit costs $1.75 for a 25 page unit. At 11-ounces it also costs $2.67 to mail, first class. When my book is included, the price for Priority Mail goes to $3.85. Media kits and books may also be sent "book rate" or 3rd class—always check rates for a package before settling on one. Shipping bags, gas to the post office and more all add to your cost of doing business.

"How much, finally, is your own time worth? That, too, is part of your cost. You may be willing to work for 'free' for yourself, but if you hire a publicist, you can expect to pay at least $50 an hour, or $500 a month, at the lowest. Chances are you'll be paying $1500 a month, for 20 hours of work, at $75 an hour. You will be charged extra for any time over that. You will need a publicist for at least three to six months and your publicist will probably charge you for out-of-pocket expenses in addition to his or her hourly or monthly rate.

"Publicity isn't really free. What's 'free' is the space you can get in newspapers and magazines and the airtime you can get on TV and radio if you approach the media in the right way, with the right information, at the right time. The material and work involved cost money. So, don't forget to face reality. Do the math."

That run-down comes from a professional. Still, I want to remind you that, compared to advertising, publicity—the art of interesting the media in ourselves or our books enough to result in no-cost ink or airtime—can be economical compared to alternatives. Later in the book, I'll talk about ideas that truly cost you nothing but time if you have a computer connected to the World Wide Web.

Hint: For more advice on basic publicity subscribe to Nicole R. Murphy's e-letter, THE BACKEND. Send an e-mail to: thebackend-subscribe@yahoogroups.com or purchase Gompertz's book, PUBLICITY ADVICE & HOW-TO HANDBOOK.

What is Branding?

Branding is not advertising, nor publicity, not even general exposure. It is the result of all your efforts, working together, how they coalesce into the publics perception of who you are, what you do.

CHJ from "Inside Retailing," Home Décor Buyer

POETS & WRITERS MAGAZINE reports that Riverhead Press' writer ZZ Packer's publishers, "Bank(ed) on…name recognition" when they sent her on a 10-city tour in 2003, something that her publisher's publicist maintains is a rare occurrence for a first-time author.

Unless you are already well known in a field and are writing a nonfiction book allied with it or you've been diligent about publicity for some time, it is unlikely that you will have the kind of public recognition Packer did. That is why *now* is better than later for beginning a publicity juggernaut and that's why your publicity efforts should *not* be aimed at your book early in the game, but rather at who you are, including your other writing.

One of the pitfalls I fell into even with a general background in PR is that I put my book—my passion—first. The day I realized that I was the one that I should be branding, instead of my book, I was putting together a business card on www.vistaprint.com. I'm not very computer savvy and I couldn't get the cover of THIS IS THE PLACE to load. I had seen business cards for real estate professionals that used thumbnail photos so I did the same. Then I muttered to myself, "Well, it's OK because I won't have to do much redesigning when and if I complete another book." Another book! Of course. When we think of books it is the author's name we think of first and, if she wrote quite a few, we are not be able to name them all.

Even after this burst of clarity, I continued to focus somewhat on the name of my book because THIS IS THE PLACE is a metaphor at several levels. It is, of course, Utah, my beloved home where I was born and raised. "Place" also refers to the farm where my protagonist goes to learn about her history and to that singular spot inside of each of us where we must go to find the courage to follow our passion. That's when I realized that I wouldn't have to change the name of my website for it, too, was a place, "the place," in fact, for learning more about me and my books.

The most savvy marketers in the world, like Coca-Cola, use several related approaches to branding themselves. (Coke is it! The Real Thing!) Branding is not necessarily an all-or-nothing proposition. If I work fervently to promote tolerance, "The Place" will be like Coke's "It" or "Thing." The public will subconsciously assign a meaning to it—the spot inside of each of us that is similar or identical to that place in every other person in the world regardless of race, religion, or gender.

I didn't plan to publish a book of creative nonfiction for my second book. It just worked out that way. I'm glad I didn't brand myself too narrowly because stationery or business cards that say "novelist" would no longer fit nor would it have fit this book—the one you are holding in your hand. My next book is a book of poetry. Again, "novelist" is wrong and "writer" seems too broad because it encompasses everything from someone who pens letters to a word can be important and an author working on a PR campaign will want to continue to refine her approach. Some writers use *nom de plumes* in order to keep their branding efforts from mucking up one another.

Here are some aspects of branding you'll want to consider:
- Decide what you want your brand to say.
  - Take into consideration what you might do in the future. Your first book may be a romance but if you choose a red hot image and decide to write a literary book, you will have chosen your "brand" unwisely.
  - Certainly you'll want to consider tie-ins to your writing or business career from your pre-book days if they will contribute to the picture you are trying to paint.
- Consider general branding as you design your website.
- Coordinate a "look" for your stationery, cards, invoices, website, and bookmarks. Do it for your voice mail greeting, your e-mail signature, the look of your instant messaging and more.

> Hint #1: Once your publisher has firmed up your title you can begin to think about a banner for it and a logo for your branding effort. If you are not graphics-savvy,

try T.C. McMullen's graphic talents: http://tc_mcmullen.tripod.com/editorialservices/.

Caveat: Wait until just before your book is released to finalize plans for large quantities of printing. You'll want to include book cover art and your ISBN into your designs.

- Begin to make yourself into an expert based on something related to your book. Choose the broadest brush possible.
- When you're making these decisions, follow your star. It will be easier to pursue a subject for which you are passionate.
- Don't be afraid to widen your path. A literary author's expertise, as an example, could easily include grammar or communication. You are building a reputation. You wouldn't want to be known only as honest among dozens of traits you aspire to.

Hint: This rule bends a bit when your book is about to be published. First you target the specific audience that will be most receptive to your work and broaden your efforts when that course has been exhausted.

Your Tagline or Mini Bio

Your tagline is as important to you as a well-tied elk hair caddis is to a fly fisherman. Without one you may have difficulty reeling in your limit.
CHJ

A tagline is personal identification that is added at the end of something your wrote or your PR message. It's shorter than what editors call a short bio. Watch the magazines and newspapers you read for examples of tagline formats. They vary in length and style. You needn't match yours to what you think a particular editor will want but it is important to "tag" one onto most everything you send out.

Keep a template of both your tagline and bio. Alter the information slightly according to where it will appear, what will interest that particular audience; add and subtract to it as you accrue experience or your focus changes. A version of a tagline might also be used as the bio paragraph in your media releases, but more about that later.

Besides your name, include as many of the following as you have access to: The URL of your website or your e-mail address, the name of your book, and a little about you.

> Hint: Rarely seen in taglines but very important is some kind of a hook (perhaps that mayfly a fisherman uses?) to encourage the reader to visit your website. This might be an offer for a free e-book, a contest or an intriguing bit of information that will pique the reader's curiosity enough to take action.

This is an example of a short bio. It was used in a flier introducing fellow authors who participated on an arts expo panel with me. It would be shortened for a tagline but the longer version gives you an idea of the kind of information that might be selected.

> **Leora G. Krygier** is the author of literary novel, FIRST THE RAVEN, and soon to be released WHEN SHE SLEEPS. She has been a finalist in the Ernest Hemingway First Novel Competition, the James Fellowship and the William Faulkner Writing Competition. Lauded for her "linguistic spell" and "poetic prose," Leora is working on her first nonfiction project. Leora is a Referee with the Superior Court of Los Angeles, and has been profiled in the *L.A. Times* for her innovative use of essay writing in juvenile dispositions. She lives in Los Angeles with her husband, two children, and the newest addition to the family, her dog, Kobi. Reach her at KRYGIERCG@aol.com. Her website is www.leorakrygier.com.

> Caveat: Editors may not always use your tagline or may not use it in the form you send it, often because of style preferences or space limitations. If they choose to publish something of yours that you have offered at no charge, they should be willing to include a tagline as a courtesy. If not, politely request that they use it. If they refuse, offer your material elsewhere next time.

The most important thing I learned as a PR professional is to brand carefully. When corporations choose a brand too narrowly, we often see them struggle to present a new image when they diversify. That is bad enough for corporations with big budgets. It can be deadly for writers with a small budget.

Your Pitch

> A pitch is an arrow that must be designed for and pointed at the target you want to reach. Deliberately aimed, it is a sales tool with a very sharp tip.
> CHJ

You may have heard about pitches, or seen them used in films made about the movie trade. From these flicks, we get the idea that pitches are pushy at best, desperate and seedy at worst. In our real world, they are only a calculated approach to selling, and selling is the cog that makes our capitalist society work. Not only are we sent a skewed image, but we are rarely told that—for a writer—there are three kinds of pitches.

1. Pitching the publishing industry:
There's the kind of pitch you toss off in a couple of perfectly wrought sentences when you must capture the interest of an agent, a publisher, a reviewer or when a reader says, "What is your book about?" Screenwriters call this pitch a logline.

2. Pitching the media:
When you want to interest an editor or producer in you or your book, you use another kind of pitch. These professionals need to see how their audience might benefit from your idea.

3. Pitching the reader:
A sales pitch is used more often with nonfiction than fiction; it tells the reader what she will gain if she reads your book or what she'll lose if she doesn't.

Pitching the Publishing Industry

> When you pitch to publishers you offer a taste of distilled water. You proffer your books essence so that whoever drinks of it is sure to want more.
> CHJ

Authors often believe they are only "shopping" their book when they approach an agent or publisher when, in reality, they have just crafted and presented their first pitch. It is true, of course, that their efforts might have been more effective if they had known exactly what they were doing. Nevertheless, most authors possess some experience as pitch writers even if they didn't know the terminology when they did it.

Because we are so familiar with our own writing or because we are so immersed in it that we don't see it clearly, writing a pitch for someone else's book is much easier than writing one for our own. As you pick up the craft of formulating a pitch from books or articles on the Web like the one at http://www.writergazette.com/articles/article131.shtml, practice using books you know well before tackling your own.

Here is an easy guideline for writing your pitch:
- Boil down your plot into three sentences or less.
- Maintain the passion you feel for your story.
- Use present tense and punchy verbs.

To learn more about pitching to the publishing industry:
- Join a screenwriters' forum. Throw out the topic of loglines and watch them go to town. Try one of your own and let them tear it apart and rebuild a thing of beauty. Here is a place to start:
  screenwriters_rule-subscribe@yahoogroups.com. With any such group it is only right for you to contribute as well as learn from others.
- Study Jonathan Treisman's audio CD workshop called THE WRITER'S HOLLYWOOD TOOLKIT. He is the President of Flatiron Films and Executive Producer of the Warner Bros. film, PAY IT FORWARD. It is available at www.writerstore.com, a site for writers and writing-related products similar to Amazon.
- Sometimes it's easier to learn from critiquing what is bad. Go to http://screenwriters.com/Moon/columns/col3.html for a quick tutorial on how to spot flaws in a logline.

> Hint: The screenwriter's craft is a fertile ground for learning marketing and writing skills that may be adapted to any kind of writing, from poetry to science fiction.

Pitching the Media
> *Journalists need you as much as you need them.*
> Anonymous

"Courage" is a key word for dealing with editors (more about that a bit later in this section). So is "relationship."

When you pitch the media you are presenting yourself or your book as something that will interest the audience of that particular editor or producer. Some ways you might do this are:

- Persuade an editor that an aspect of your personality or life (one that is related to your book in some way) would make a good feature article.
- Convince a TV or radio producer that you or your book would interest her viewers or listeners.
- Sell yourself to the media as an expert on a subject related to your book.
- Offer yourself as an interviewee to hosts or journalists who specialize in profiles.
- Entice a reviewer to review your book.
- Convince a webmaster or editor to feature you in a myriad of other ways, like Author of the Month.

The time or space you have to catch a prospect's attention is limited. The journalist needs to know what you can offer that will make her job easier. Remember the 12 "No-Nos" at the beginning of this book? Those who work in the media do not exist to give you free publicity because you want or need it. The journalist wants to know what about you or you book will fascinate her audience. This might include:

- Information that is brand new to her audience.
- Something that will solve a problem for her audience.
- Something that will entertain her audience.
- Something that will involve the audience emotionally (a human interest story).

Start your pitch quickly; make the media person aware of a problem that you can solve for her, then—just as rapidly—outline how information about you or your book is the solution to that problem. She won't want your life's story or a synopsis of your book until she's convinced that she *needs* you.

It is obvious that formulating a great pitch is easier for a how-to or other book of nonfiction. It is more difficult for writers of fiction but don't let anyone tell you it's impossible. It does require more analysis, more creativity to do so.

How *you* might be interesting:

- Hometown reporters want to know they have a published author living in their town.
- Journals for seniors are interested if you are over 55; almost everyone will be interested if you are very young.
- Perhaps you've changed careers midstream; that might interest editors of business magazines or business sections.
- You might have a women's or men's angle that will work for gender-related periodicals.
- Are you a vegetarian and how did that affect your creative process?
- Is your book controversial? Are you? Some say there is no such thing as bad publicity. The exposure and sales of Richard Clarke's book, AGAINST ALL ENEMIES, was helped considerably by controversy as well is its well-timed release.

Heat up a cup of tea or go to your local latté parlor to make a list of all the aspects of your personality and life in a relaxed atmosphere. Tie each of them to an angle that will be **beneficial** to journalists in specialized areas. (See a section later in this chapter that discusses benefits, a model used to sell to editors and readers.)

How your book might fill a reporter's need:

- Some editors like the idea that a novel is set in their locale.
- Are there any premises or themes in your fiction that shed light on what is happening in the news? A book that exposes the corrosive nature of intolerance after 9/11, as an example.
- Is there a literary interest? You might have written in an unusual cross-genre that will be news for periodicals marketed to authors.
- Is there a strong similarity in your work to a film or book that everyone is talking about? Sometimes reporters like to tie one to another and reviewers like to pack reviews of two or more similar books into one commentary.

Avoid missing the obvious by setting up a brainstorming session with three or more who have read your book. No idea is too silly. Nothing is to be repressed. You may be surprised at how many angles come from such a group effort.

Just so you realize that this can be done, all of the above ideas were used for my first novel, THIS IS THE PLACE. I thought of it as a literary novel but found that it also fit into "little bit" categories: a little bit historical; a little bit saga; a little bit romance; a little bit feminist; a little bit women's; a little bit western. I also found that, by virtue of my age, there were lots of aspects of my past life and former careers that worked well for editors.

Back to that "courage" thing. Too many times we rely on mail, e-mail and faxes to get the job done because we are squeamish about meeting with media face-to-face or by phone. Think of such close contact as bringing a caring attitude to your association with the media.

Why do publishers put the pictures of authors on the flaps of dust covers? Because human beings relate to faces. Although editors try to be impartial, they are only human; they relate best on a one-to-one basis just like readers or anyone else. You will have more success if you get to know your media contacts at close range. When that's impossible, include your picture in your media kit, just as your publisher has learned to do.

Try to script your first contact with an editor. Make it a fact finding mission so that she is aware that you want to make her job easier. Try to arrange to see her in her office. Let's pretend as if you're working on your first, big event—your book launch. Ask questions like these:

- "How can I help with pre-event coverage?" You'd rather have coverage before the event than after for obvious reasons, but you word this so that the benefits to the editor are visible.
- "May I give you photos to accompany your stories?" By the way, it doesn't hurt to make a contact with the head of your local paper's photography department, either. I wrote to ask her for a copy of a picture she had taken of me, complimented her on it and cc'd that praise to her superior. All sincere. And helpful to both of us, I hope.
- "How are photos best submitted? Electronically? Professional slick copies? Color or black or white?"
- "Would you be interested in learning about the remarkable people associated with my launch as the subject of a feature article?" When an editor uses this kind of feature material she usually credits you and your event.

- "I would love to have you attend as an honored guest. Do you need a map to help you find the event? A parking pass? Reserved seating?" If the editor accepts, formally introduce her to the audience during your presentation.

> Caveat: Match the editor to the kind of coverage you're seeking. Study the newspaper's roster for clues. Call TV and radio stations and ask the receptionist to direct you. Check websites. Pronounce names correctly. You may want to contact more than one editor for a given event. Here are some possibilities:
> - Calendar Editor.
> - Feature Editor.
> - Weekend Editor.
> - Book Review Editor.
> - Assignment Editor (usually TV).
> - City Editor.
> - A Beat Reporter (These can range from business to arts and entertainment.)

Here is how one of my early gurus, Raleigh Pinskey Raleigh@promoteyourself.com) pitches the media by phone. As you can see, she incorporates elements of a formal pitch, but, conversationally, it is quite different. If you rehearse Raleigh's approach out loud, it moves along so quickly it feels like three or four lines:

> "Hello, I'm the author of 101 WAYS TO PROMOTE YOURSELF: TRICKS OF THE TRADE TO TAKE CHARGE OF YOUR OWN SUCCESS. The book is published by Harper Collins/Quill and has sold close to 100,000 copies.
> **(Note how she establishes credibility.)**

> "I show your audience how they can get more than just those '15 minutes of fame,' plus money-making tips, and ways they can be a household name, online and offline locally or globally.
> **(Here Raleigh lists benefits. You'll learn more about these in the next section.)**

> "I've been helping business people to fame and fortune for 25 years. I've worked with Sting, McCartney, Blondie, KISS, Chicken Soup for the Soul, Fit For Life Solution, and hundreds of mouse and mortar businesses.
> **(Here she tosses in more credibility plus some razzle-dazzle.)**

"My name is Raleigh Pinskey and I would love to be a guest on your show so both of us can help take the members of your audience to their next level of success. **(Notice how she asks for exactly what she wants.)**

"(I wait until the end to say my name because it's not important until they want to book me. Why take the chance of losing their interest in the beginning with unimportant information and small talk. I go right to the chase.)"
(Learn more about Raleigh at www.PromoteYourself.com and www.RaleighSeminars.com)

You may or may not yet have the glitzy credits to your name that Raleigh has; use what you have (some of your credentials may be vocation oriented) and what is appropriate. You'll gather more as you become more acclaimed.

Pitching to Sell: Benefits and Consequences

Do you, while receiving benefits from me and resting under my shade, dare to describe me as useless, and unprofitable?

Aesop

Your sales pitch makes your audience aware of the benefits of the product you offer—in this case your book—or makes them fear the consequences of not using it. Aesop knew that those who see its usefulness are more than likely to appreciate it; they may even be reluctant to be negative about it.

When I owned retail stores I told my new sales associates that people shop because they want to buy something. I was surprised that I had to give them this lecture but past experience told me it was necessary. "Shopping makes them happy," I'd say. "When we shop, our companion may ask, 'How did you do?' If the item isn't a good fit, if the shopper doesn't find something she just 'loves,' both the inquirer and the shopper are disappointed." It is no different when customers are thumbing through the books on shelves at a bookstore; your book's cover is a silent sales associate. Of course, if you happen to be a presenter or are signing, you shouldn't be at all silent.

Once crafted, your sales pitch is used verbally, on the back cover of books and in advertisements. To properly compose your pitch:

- Identify the aspects of your book that will most interest a reader in a given time or market and the distinguishing features of your book.
- Write them down.
- Turn these features into statements that show how a reader will benefit.
- A nonfiction example would be: "This book builds the confidence necessary to promote."
- A frequently-used fiction example is: "This book keeps readers turning pages late into the night." I'm sure you can do better than this.
- Now add a little cayenne to those benefits, make them hot. Make them sparkle.
- Stow a variety of pitches on your computer. Utilize the appropriate one in your:
  - Media releases
  - Fliers
  - Posters for events like fairs and book signings.
  - To add urgency to taglines and other forms of exposure.

Using consequences instead of benefits is espoused by Dan Seidman in THE DEATH OF 20ᵀᴴ CENTURY SELLING. His book shows readers how to turn benefits around to scare the beejeebees out of prospective readers and tell them the horrors that will befall them if they don't buy your book. You already hold THE FRUGAL BOOK PROMOTER in your hands but, if I were trying to sell you using consequences, I would tell you that your book will expire in the piles of remaindered and shredded books—some 1/3 of all books published each year—if you don't promote yourself and your book early.

Paul Hartunian (http://www.systemdating.com/author.html), the author of HOW TO FIND THE LOVE OF YOUR LIFE IN 90 DAYS OR LESS, used a twist on the consequence approach in one of his media releases. He used a short list of "Don'ts" and included: "The worst place to go on a first date—go here and you'll probably never get a second date." He tormented the editors by not giving them the answer to the question he posed. The recipient of such a release is not only curious but also is aware that his audience will be, too. It's a sure bet that Hartunian's release was effective.

It is easier for writers of nonfiction to use consequences but fiction writers should try to find a consequence to use in at least one of their pitches. In 2002, I might have told prospective readers that their enjoyment of the winter Olympics would be severely impaired if they didn't read THIS IS THE PLACE so they would understand the history and culture of the city in which the games were set that year.

> Hint: Select benefit, consequence or both when they fit the occasion, not when they feel forced.

> Caveat: Occasionally a headline is used in conjunction with a pitch. Carefully shape it so that it holds its own in the glare of your powerful pitch.

Encourage the Flow of Valuable PR Advice

> SPAM is not the biggest danger; censorship is far more destructive to the work of a writer (or publicist). If she has a dearth of information or if it is inaccurate, she will wither and die.
> CHJ

As a writer you know that information is vital to what you put on paper, and how you put it there. You now may need to reach out to new resources to get what you need. Read what comes to you; even unlikely messages can lead you to other contacts.

Use several good search engines. Join e-groups and chat rooms where fellow writers congregate to discuss writing and promotion. Ditto for groups with interests that are related to the subject matter of your book. Subscribe to e-zines (online magazines and newsletters). You'll be able to submit releases and articles to them but you'll also learn from them. Forge relationships with these editors, too. Let all these possibilities come right to your screen. You won't even have to tear open an envelope.

Here is a starter kit:
- Joan Stewart calls her newsletter THE PUBLICITY HOUND for good reason and, though she is interested in

publicity for all kinds of businesses, she doesn't neglect authors. To receive copies send a blank email to joinpublicitytips@lists.publicityhound.com.

> Hint: Practice some of the publicity skills you will learn in this book on her. She may publish your ideas along with your book's name and a link. She often teams up with experts when her readers will benefit.

- Subscribe to PUBINSIDER MONTHLY for free publishing, PR and some services like lists of independent bookstores that you can purchase. Reach Editor Jeffrey Bowen at pubinsider@earthlink.net.
- Marketing sage John Kremer has revived his Book Marketing Tip of the Week. Send an e-mail to: JohnKremer@bookmarket.com to subscribe.

Chapter 3: Build Your Media Kit Before You Need It

An authors media kit is an enticing tool box for any editor or producer who opens it. It should provide any gizmo she needs to get a story out fast and easy.

CHJ

A well-designed media kit is a sales tool and insures your contact that you are qualified, but it is also a resource. It makes it easy for a reporter, editor or producer to write the news, review your book, do an interview or write a feature story. Editors today have more responsibility—do more in less time—than they ever have. It is only natural that they tend to favor news that is supported so well it nearly writes itself.

We're going to get biological so that you can begin your media kit today. We're going to build the skeleton of your kit so that as you add tendons and muscles to your credentials, you have a place to store the information. A strong structure that has been fleshed out as you become more and more qualified (and as you have time to work on it) will require only a little grooming before your publicity campaign starts in earnest. Having the bones in place will help you visualize the progress of your writing career as well as help you select the promotions that will best suit your needs.

Your Media Contact List

Another friend, another door...

Chinese Proverb

Your contact list is not part of your media kit but without it your kit will be useless. Certainly you can wait until just before your book is released to purchase or research information for it, but if you do, the many contacts that you will be making and ideas or experiences you are about to encounter may be lost.

We'll work on the details of a media contact list later in the book but for now, break out your data base program and start saving essential information on anyone you meet who might be interested in you or your book. When in doubt, make a temporary entry. Your list can be edited later; your goal is not to lose anyone. When I slip up, I'm sure to regret it later. Be sure to include a cell for codes such as:

- Personal-PRS.
- Writing-WRT.
- Media-TV, RDIO, PRS.
- Professional-PROF.
- Librarians-LIB.
- Bookstores-BKST.
- Catalogs-CTLG.
- Clubs CLB or SOC (for social).
- Other Support-OTHR.

The Media Release

> A compelling media release is like a good quarterback; even if he can make a perfect pass, he needs teamwork to be consistently effective.
> CHJ, from "15 Commandments for Getting Free Publicity" in the Creative Line

A media release is often effective all by itself, especially if news is sent frequently to an editor. However, if you want to shout out great news, explain complicated news, or supply the kind of support to the media that makes it hard for them to ignore your story, your release needs backup. That's when the release will become part—albeit one of the most important parts—of a media kit.

Press Releases are Really Media Releases

Media releases come in all shapes, sizes and formats but that doesn't mean you can write your own ticket. In the next section I tell you how to fit the pieces of a release puzzle together. I'll warn you now, you can drive yourself crazy looking up different samples, different guidelines on the Web and elsewhere. Follow the directions I give you and keep a headache at bay.

However, if you choose to try different formats, do not deviate from calling your release a "media release" rather than a "press release" in your e-mail subject line (along with a pithy title), as the header for your release and in your conversations with editors. "Press release" is a term used several decades ago and marks you as a novice or woefully behind the times.

Building Your Media Release:
Writing a media release is less like manipulating a Rubik's cube and more like putting together a puzzle—the kind of puzzle with big, easy pieces that you could do when you were only three.

If you've written a book, you can master a media release. If you have your release assembled before you need it or before a publicist's fee-clock starts ticking, you'll save a lot of money and time. Start now. Leave blanks where you don't have the information you need. Save it in your computer under "Media Kit for (The Working Title of Your Book.)"

It will help if you read the sample release in the appendix of this book. It is a visual aid for the work you will be doing, like the cover of a puzzle's box. Here are ten puzzle parts to fit together for a media release:

Puzzle Piece 1:
The header consists of five lines below your stationery's letterhead.
- The first line says **M E D I A   R E L E A S E**. Use caps, large type, bold face, 18 point Arial typeface with a space between each letter, three spaces between the words. Justify it on the left of your page.
- Double space. Enter **CONTACT:** in 14 point, Arial caps, left justified. If you hire a publicist, this would be her contact information; use your own if you send the release yourself. Include a name, phone, fax and e-mail address, each on its own line. Revert back to upper and lower case for the details. Include this information even if it is in your letterhead.

Puzzle Piece 2:
Release information goes one space beneath the contact information.

- Type in **For Immediate Release** in 12 point bold Times New Roman, left justified. Change this information only if there is a very good reason for doing so. In that case this line would read: **For Release After 00/00/00**. Both available space and timeliness is an issue for editors. Don't limit them with a specific date unless you must.

Puzzle Piece 3:
Your headline is centered in 16 point Arial bold.
- Your headline should seize an editor or producer's attention so she doesn't scrunch the release into a ball and toss it. Study headlines in the newspaper. Feature the most newsworthy (original, unique or charity-driven) element of your release in your headline.

Puzzle Piece 4:
The lead is simple and brief.
- It is the first sentence in the body of your release. State who, how, where and what. You will later learn how to make this line more appealing to editors, but until that can be mastered, a straightforward, old-fashioned journalist's lead is better than one that screams inexperience. Check to be sure that the "when" includes the day of the week and the date. A rudimentary example is: **"*Shades of Iris,* a novel by Marlena Day, was released by Schuster Arrow Press on August 1."**

Puzzle Piece 5:
The body of the release follows, single spaced.
- Leave a space between paragraphs. Do not indent. Mention the single most newsworthy aspect of your event in the paragraph after the lead: **"This is Day's first novel."**
- The next paragraph lists the author's most important credentials, including her hometown if the release is being sent to the local press.

Puzzle Piece 6:
Your logline or pitch for you book comes next.
- You may have already written your first pitch. It's that mini-synopsis of your book meant to snare an editor's attention.

Caveat: If this is the release to be used in your media kit, use this puzzle piece as part of Puzzle Piece # 5.

Puzzle Piece 7:
Your permanent promotional paragraph comes next.
- Put this mini-bio together once and it may only need an occasional update. It gives important background on the author. **"Day has been writing ad copy and promotional pieces since she started her own party planning business in 1988..."** Don't worry if you don't have much writing-oriented information to include here. You might use professional information or leave it blank. You'll learn how to build your credentials later in this chapter.
- Do not include your hobbies unless they have something to do with the subject of the book.
- Use this paragraph in every release you write.
- Add credentials to this template as they build.

Puzzle Piece 8:
Your close is easy.
- Type in a similar line to this: *"Shades of Iris"* **is available in bookstores or online at** www.Amazon.com.**"**
- On another line type in **"Learn more at:** www.????.com.**"** That's your website address which you'll eventually use as a sales tool for both readers and the press.
- Type in three pound signs, **"###,"** and center them to signify the end of the release.

Puzzle Piece 9:
Media kit, photos and website are mentioned next in parentheses.
- This is not part of the body of your release so put it in 8 point bold, Times New Roman, centered. **"A media kit and photos are available on request."**

Puzzle Piece 10:
Save what you have done as a sample or template for your media kit. You'll be tweaking this format every time you do something newsworthy.

You may choose to mail, fax or e-mail your release or use a combination of the three.

- If you fax, include a cover sheet to direct it to the proper editor. This will usually be the features or managing editor. For radio and TV, it will be the producer of each show.
- Be certain you have the current editor's name and that it is spelled correctly.
- If you have photos, send a release by USPS or Fed Ex at some point in your campaign. Because many editors will not open e-mail attachments, you'll want them to have a picture which might convince them better than words alone. If you are not sending the release with a kit, use envelopes to match your letterhead and print each address using the envelope feeder on your printer rather than handwriting them.

Here are some techniques to make your media release a success:

- When your release is complete, it should be one page or less. (Don't cheat by using a smaller typeface. If your release is too long, go back and edit. You are sure to find some inflated puzzle pieces that got into your box accidentally.)
- Go back and remove all the high-falutin' adjectives. In media releases "awesome" and "magnificent" are four-letter words.
- No opinions allowed. To be more realistic, no *blatant* opinions.
- Punch up the headline.

> Example: "Noted Author Examines Little White Lies in Fact and Fiction." "Noted" is opinion of sorts but it works reasonably well in a headline if it is true in some sense and that opinion is verified in the body of the release. The idea in this headline is irregular enough to capture an editor's attention, but not so outrageous that a more conservative editor will be put off. "New Website Opens Its Doors," or "Local Woman Writes Book," is an example of humdrum.

- If you have a blurb from a professional or an expert that might convince an editor of your stature, slice it into the release as one of your puzzle pieces.

Example: "Dale Barton, President of Armand, Busch and Co., says, "This is the year's definitive book on world demographics.""

- If someone is available to proofread your release for typos, use that second pair of eyes. Microsoft Word's spell and grammar checker is helpful, not perfect.

The hard work is done. Leave blanks where you don't have information. Fill in details as they become available. Fine-tune before you send the release out.

Advanced Techniques for Leads

I've given you the basics for writing a release above. You may want to tackle a more enticing lead than the usual how, where, when and why lead. Here are a couple of approaches that might work but do not deviate from the basics until you are sure of your footing.

- **Tried and True:** Most media releases use a conservative, professional lead—even for a book that lends itself to something far more exciting—that looks like this:

  "Peter Morton, publisher of Tyr Publishing, Los Angeles, has signed a contract for CHRISTMAS COOKIES ARE FOR GIVING with longtime Palm Springs resident, Kristin J. Johnson. This book, a combination of cookbook and book of inspiration, will be released in August of this year."

- **Using a Modified Benefit Lead:** To tackle something more daring and probably more effective, write a lead that points out the benefits of your book or warns of the dangers inherent in ignoring it. Here is an example of a lead that uses a little scare along with a bit of benefit.

  "Carolyn Howard-Johnson, author of two award-winning books, spent the last four years stepping into dangerous publicity potholes. She shares her hard-won expertise on publicizing books with the release of THE FRUGAL BOOK PROMOTER, which will be released by Star Publish in August of this year."

When a lead like this is used, some of the essential details that normally are part of a lead will need to be moved down to the next paragraph. This may misalign that puzzle you are building but you're a writer. You will figure it out.

- **Other Choices:** A variation that works well for novels as well as nonfiction are the use of a poignant quote from your book or a spot-on blurb from a celebrity that praises your book. Place it just above your traditional lead. Indent and italicize it.

Follow-up

Follow-up is as important to clinching a publicity deal as a homerun at the bottom of the 9th inning is to the World Series. When your release or your kit has been sitting on your editor's desk for about five working days, phone to see if she received it, ask if she has any questions and be prepared to pitch a different angle on the story to her.

Fax or e-mail a slightly different release or announcement after you have sent out your kit. (See the next section.)

Editors Love Media Announcements

...men give us most rarely that which we really want...
Frances Power Cobb

Media *announcements* are shorter and sometimes, to the eyes of an editor, sweeter than media *releases*. Use announcements to notify editors of an upcoming event. Use them as an introduction to a planned media blitz of well-spaced releases, each touting a different angle. Media announcements read like bare-bones invitations. Include:

- The term "Media Announcement" as a header.
- A captivating headline.
- Use a pithy lead.
- Follow up with the place, time, date and contact information.
- For more help use Kevin Nunley's media announcement creator at: http://InternetWriters.com/release.htm.

Your About the Author Page

> The author himself is the best judge of his own performance; none has so deeply meditated on the subject; none is so sincerely interested in the event...
>
> Edward Gibbon, from MEMOIRS OF MY LIFE (1796).

Your "About the Author" page in your media kit is one that only you—even with the best publicist on hire—can do. It is a short, third person piece about you.

This page contains information similar to that which your publisher uses on the flyleaf of your book's dust cover or on the back cover of your book. However, it is better if it adds some new information to that biography.

Editors glean both personal and professional information about you from this page. That is why even authors who are adverse to publicity include a bit about where they live or something about their hobbies. This page may be as short as a paragraph or long enough to fill up a page.

Until your relevant credentials grow, you may prefer to title this a "Mini Biography." Later you can elect to add a longer "About the Author" page but keep your "Mini Biography" as part of your kit. An editor may find it convenient to have a choice. The idea is to provide editors with the information they need, in the format that will be most helpful to them. Here are some tips:

- Use wide margins in a clear font of at least 12 points, single spaced, less than one page long.
- Avoid clichés. One of the most common is saying that you "always" wanted to write. I made this mistake myself and cringe every time I see material that utilized this old version of my author's page.
- Select what you tell about yourself with an eye to both branding and to your book. Readers of a how-to book on investing or fiction set on Wall Street would find that the author was a financial advisor relevant. If what he wrote had no relationship to the world of money, that expert in finance might do better to highlight some other aspect of his life.

Your Awards and Publications

> On slow news days, editors see words like "prize" and "award" as unset jewels. They will not care if they are semiprecious stones or the finest cut diamonds because they know that either will add luster to a story.
>
> CHJ

Whether you identify awards and publications on the same page in your media kit or use separate pages is a choice you can make. At first—until you have a very long list of either awards or places your work has been published—you may want to include these on the same page because, in some ways, a published article is an award, a kind of affirmation of the quality of your work.

You probably need no introduction to the page but organize the listings similarly to the way you would a resume. Place the "Awards" first on the page, "Publications" next. Within these categories, list your most recent achievements first because, as your career progresses, the more current ones tend to be more prominent.

> Caveat: If you should be talented and lucky enough to win an important prize, let it shine on a page by itself. Use wide margins, perhaps even a decorative border to highlight it. Emblazon this award on anything you can, your business card, the inscription on your promotional gift, your media release and the next edition of your book's cover.

Your Sample Review

> Critics are sentinels in the grand army of letters, stationed at the corners of newspapers and reviews, to challenge every new author.
>
> Henry Wadsworth Longfellow

Many of those in the media you or your publicity person contact will be as interested in finding a brilliant new angle or writing their own captivating story as they are in the worth of your book. Regardless of why they are interested, most editors will use the review you enclose in your media kit as an indicator of the quality of your work. As soon as you have a positive review, add it to your media kit but make a heading for that page now as a reminder. Once you have a review to fill the space:

- Ask permission from the reviewer to add it to your media kit as a sample.
- Note where the review originally appeared and the reviewer's name near the top of the page.
- If a headline is not part of the original review, provide one that is true to the intent of the reviewer.
- Some independent reviewers will allow you to offer their reviews to editors for reprint. If you have permission, ask the new publishers to print the review complete using the critic's byline and tagline. Both this request and permission to reprint the review is noted at the top of your review page above the headline.
- You might choose to include two reviews. If so, each should focus on different aspects of your book; you may also provide one short review and a longer one to accommodate different styles or space requirements of different editors.

> Hint #1: If you don't yet have a review, substitute a mini synopsis. Use active verbs, third person and don't give away the ending. Make your synopsis a big enough tease that even a jaded reviewer or editor will want to read your book.
>
> Hint #2: If you have a review that isn't as good as you'd like, resist the temptation to use a positive excerpt. Reviewers and editors will not be fooled. Know also that media people know a review that is critical of one aspect of your book is more credible than one that raves on excessively; editors suspect that a pie-in-the-sky review was probably written by your mother.
>
> Hint #3: If you want to extract raves from a review, use them on your "Praise" page where gleaning the best of the best from reviews and elsewhere is acceptable.
>
> Caveat: Use no more than two reviews in your media kit.

Your List of Appearances

> It is only shallow people who do not judge by
> appearances. The true mystery of the world is the
> visible, not the invisible.
>
> Oscar Wilde

Just like the people of depth in Wilde's world, you will be judged by the kit you present to the media, but more specifically your "Appearances" page. Radio and TV producers look for authors with not only expertise but someone with enough *presence* to make them proud; after all, their reputation is at stake. This page isn't as important to those in the print media but they may still be impressed by it.

Because this page is so important, scour your past to find some indicator that you will be comfortable before a camera or mike. Here are some possibilities:

- Did you study drama in college? High school?
- Have you taken a Dale Carnegie course?
- Ever been on a debate team?
- Led seminars or been a panelist as part of your business experience?
- Acted as an instructor in the education or business worlds?
- Been a model? Taken an acting class? Been in a play?
- Read an excerpt from your book at a signing? Been a panelist at a book fair?

Stellar credentials are not essential. Most authors or "experts" are not professional speakers; you only want to show that you can handle the job. Note something like, **"Modeling and debate experience. References on request,"** will do nicely as the start.

If you have nothing for this page, insert an empty page with only the title on it. The universe has a very nice way of filling empty spaces, meeting positive demands head on. In the meantime, take a speech class. You'll find a thousand reasons in your future to be grateful you did.

> Caveat: If you don't have a suitable entry for any given page in your media kit, remove that page before sending your kit out.

Your Sample Interview

> My opposition [to interviews] lies in the fact that
> offhand answers have little value or grace of
> expression, and that such oral give and take helps
> to perpetuate the decline of the English language.
> James Thurber

A "Sample Interview" is a text of an interview, imagined or real, that a reporter might use to glean questions for his own interview. You have seen the interview format in PEOPLE MAGAZINE and others. It looks like a transcript of questions and answers. The sample interview in your media kit is your chance to combat the inferior quality of interviews—both the questions and answers—that Thurber describes.

Many authors reproduce one of the interviews that appeared in a publication for their kits. They believe it is preferable to writing their own because a reprint is attributed to the publications in which they appeared. If the media or reporter is one of stature, that can be an advantage; a little name-dropping in a media kit is essential, not a social faux pas.

Having said that, if the interviews available to you do not focus on content you prefer (and I, along with Thurber believe that they usually don't!) you may write the questions that *you* think offer the best opportunity for presenting yourself and your book in the light you envision for it. Of course, your answers (also written by you) will be witty, entertaining and, preferably, short. Some reporters will use the interview you present verbatim; others may adapt your questions to their needs and others will ignore them. Writing your own interview gives you (or your publicist) as much control as possible over the interview process.

Nothing keeps you from listing the esteemed reporters who have interviewed you at the bottom of the page, mentioning them in one of your interview's answers or including them on your "Appearances" page. A media kit should follow guidelines closely but the content is indeed more flexible than the inscription on your great grandfather's headstone.

> Hint: You could substitute an FAQ (Frequently Asked
> Questions) section for a sample interview if you are

writing it yourself, perhaps the same one you will eventually use for your website.

Your First Person Essay

> I almost always urge people to write in the first person... Writing is an act of ego and you might as well admit it.
>
> William Zinsser, from ON WRITING WELL

Zinsser might well have mentioned that it is disingenuousness to remove the author from the telling of her own story by using third person. After all, the author is the ultimate expert on herself and the pronoun "I" is not a dirty word.

Because you're a writer you are probably aware of how frequently first person essays are used in the press. Some newspapers actually label a column on the left hand side of their front page "First Person." You'll see them in the LOS ANGELES TIMES called "First Column." You'll find some in the same location on the front page of their food and other sections, too. A widely distributed magazine called GUIDEPOSTS (www.guideposts.com) is dedicated to this kind of writing. Such essays are often used in anthologies, collections of essays and more.

You have dozens of stories to tell about yourself and probably tell them occasionally in conversation. Perhaps you already have a written one; your media kit will be more complete if you include a narrative focused on the themes that drive you as a writer, how you came to writing or subjects related to the theme, setting or other aspects of your book. Present your first person essay in your kit complete with permission to reprint it exactly as you submit it.

Sometimes when authors write about themselves, their narrative becomes stilted. A first person essay should be lively and full of anecdote and dialogue. Eventually you may want to have several different essays or versions of your essay stowed away in your computer because different publications focus on different subjects. One of my essays talks about my bout with cancer and how my search for health brought me back to writing after a long hiatus. Another is about my struggle with repression of women in the 60s and how that affected my early writing career. One tells of my love of yoga, and—you guessed it—how that helps my writing. Another, my interest in travel. One relates how writing has affected my life as a senior. I switch out the essay I include in my media kit depending on where I am sending the kit. It doesn't take me long to rewrite one of these (dare I say "canned" essays?) if a new opportunity presents itself and none of my previously written pieces are appropriate.

In your media kit you'll want to:
- Label this page "First Person Story."
- Keep it from 700 to 1000 words; staple the pages together.
- Use an attention-getting title.
- Place a free-use permission statement under the title.
- Include your byline and tagline (see chapter two).
- Try to include the title of your book in the body of the piece but be sure it is an integral part of the story, not an obvious add-on.

A well-written first person essay may be reprinted by an editor exactly as it is presented. Sometimes a reporter will call for more information or for permission to rewrite it under her byline (the answer is always "Yes!!") Other times it may trigger interest in using you in a story but the editor may choose an entirely different angle.

> Caveat: If you hire a publicist, she may not use first person essays in her kits, especially if she doesn't have authors as clients. It may be up to you to convince her of its importance. You, after all, are the client. She should accommodate your suggestion.

Your Available Seminars List

> The hearing ear is always found close to the speaking tongue.
> Ralph Waldo Emerson

Those in the business world who are excellent speakers are among the most successful; those in the book biz who can and will speak find they are in a better position to make big ripples in the publishing world. If fear keeps you from sharing your expertise, I urge you to take a baby step toward overcoming it for the sake of your personal growth and the success of your publicity campaign.

Settling on your seminar topics is similar to searching for angles that will interest editors. Examine every aspect of your book. Rediscover the passion that obligated you to write it in the first place. Come up with at least two topics that appeal to audiences with diverse tastes. These might include a writing workshop, a moderated panel on publishing, or a seminar on the premise of your book.

You needn't write your speech but do consider whether you will have (or can research) enough material to make the ones you offer successful if you should get a speaking "gig." Write a catchy title and an intriguing pitch for each topic. Use the skills you learned in chapter two for writing loglines, pitches and beguiling synopses of your book.

> Hint: That you have this page in your media kit marks you as a professional and indicates to the media that you have presentation skills that they need even if you choose not to pursue speaking as an essential part of your campaign.

Your Fellow Expert List

> An expert is a man who has made all the mistakes which can be made in a very narrow field.
> Neils Bohr, Danish physicist

When you include a list of experts who compliment your expertise—ones who are charismatic and know how to work as a team—you mark yourself as a professional and make it oh, so easy for an editor or producer to style a story or segment in which you are an integral part.

Here are some quick tips for your expert list:
- Your expert list should be on a page by itself, very brief, just the facts, ma'am.
- Include at least one expert who holds an opinion different from yours and make this clear in the way he or she is listed.
- Include contact information for each entry and a one sentence description of what makes him or her an expert.

Other Media Kit Items

Bear with me, good boy, I am much forgetful.
Shakespeare, from JULIUS CEASAR

You are building your media kit now so that it can act as a filing cabinet for the credentials you are about to amass. Each page is a folder of sorts. If you are as forgetful as I, you will not remember certain elements of this project without a reminder. Experts on organization suggest you handle any single process as rarely as possible so having a page for "Other Items" will mean that you won't have to search your whole kit when you remember that it should include something that starts with a "P" but can't remember what the devil "P" stands for. This "Other Items" is a string around your finger; remember to cross each item off this page as you complete each task.

Once you've signed your book's contract you'll begin to accrue these enclosures for your kit:
- Your picture (see chapter 13).
- Your business or sales card
- Your galley or Advanced Reader Copy (see chapter eight).
- A color picture of your book cover (see chapter 11).

Most items on this list are essentials but they needn't be. Here is an example of a memory-jogger I once put on my list that I never got around to doing. I wanted to make a tip sheet of sorts called "Ten Weird and Wonderful Facts About Utah" that I would include in my media kit complete with permission to print it. This note in my sample kit tends to nag me but it is my prerogative to ignore it just as it will be yours. That I kept this note, however, helped me to design a line of questioning for a late night radio host, so it didn't go completely to waste.

> Hint: Feel free to throw in any idea that comes to mind. This one page in your sample kit will be for your eyes only.

Media Kit Materials

Suitability should be considered in choosing...paper, as well as in choosing a piece of furniture for a house.
Emily Post

When you frequent writers' sites, you'll read much about attracting the attention of editors with all manner of exotic packaging for your media kit. Only if the subject of your book demands an outlandish presentation or if this "cutesy" approach is so much part of your personality you feel comfortable with it should you follow the advice of the crazies. Creativity is a good thing but keep your branding—read that reputation—in mind.

You now have the frame of your kit ready to put into a two-pocket presentation folder, the kind with tiny diagonal slits in the fold-up pocket portion to accommodate a business card. Purchase an inexpensive one at your local stationery shop to serve as your sample kit.

If you handle your own PR, you'll want to buy enough folders to accommodate your first year's needs and you'll want to choose a better quality than most office warehouses stock. Wait until you can project the number you'll need reasonably accurately. They are much cheaper if purchased in bulk. Here is your game plan:

- If you are not artistic, you might ask a friend who is a graphic artist, someone at your local Kinko's or use the templates of an online printer like www.vistaprint.com to help you design your folder and kit.
- Choose a color for your folder that works well with your book cover.
- Choose paper for the innards that is lineny or heavy enough that an editor will notice.

> Hint: Multi-colored ink adds to the cost of any print job so try to design your folder and contents using one color ink on contrasting paper.

> Hint #2: The information in your kit will change rapidly; print out only what you'll need for any given mailing.

How to Assemble Your Kit

Public-Relations specialists make flower arrangements of the facts, placing them so the wilted and less attractive petals are hidden by sturdy blooms.
Alan Harrington, Author

Your media kit is not a one-size fits all presentation. The basics—like the folder—will probably remain the same, but you may assemble your kit differently from one mailing occasion to the next. You've been building a sample kit. Keep it saved on your hard drive, of course, but also keep an old fashioned hard copy. It will:

- Be your safety valve in case of a computer meltdown.
- Be both a sample and reminder for building other kits when the time comes.
- Aid in experimentation. In real life you can play with each page and part of a media kit like a puzzle, rearrange it to its best advantage depending upon the branch of the media you are sending it to and the angle you want to emphasize. By doing this you can increase your kit's impact.

Generally, you'll assemble your material so that the news release is on top in the right hand pocket. Order the other segments behind it, the most pertinent first. Your "About the Author" page will probably come next, your "Awards" page and then... You decide this order by determining which pages will most effectively convince an editor of your newsworthiness.

At the left, place your picture, your promotion gift, if any, a copy of your book cover and your book, if you are including one. If you have decided to include anything that is not in the realm of the usual media kit fare, it would go on this side.

The front of the kit usually sports your book's cover art; for THIS IS THE PLACE I chose a five-word "pitch," printed it in a nostalgic font on parchment and glued it to the front of my kit. There is not really a right or wrong kind of presentation folder cover as long as it is professionally rendered.

As a courtesy, attach a cover letter to the outside of the kit with a paperclip—usually one that contributes to the design either by shape or color. This letter should be a brief and not necessarily formal introduction that will pique an editor's interest.

> Hint: To save time later, shop stationers or office supply businesses when you are "out and about" or surfing the Web. Your ideas about what you want will change as you compare prices and learn what is available. Media kits are diverse as the covers and subjects of books.

> Check out your "business to business" phone book for suppliers if your needs are exotic.

I experiment regularly with the way my kit is set up. I use Word's Insert/Break functions to separate each page from one another. Though I keep my electronic pages in the order in which I most frequently use them, I don't number them. That way, I can choose to change the page order or print a single page without making adjustments to my header.

Each page of your kit should include contact information, either simple ones like those you would find on a thesis paper or designed as letterheads.

> Caveat: A designed letterhead on each page may increase the time it takes to send your kit by attachment. Also, don't attach anything to e-mails unless an editor requests it.

> Alert for novice computer users: Back up your media release file—it should fit on a floppy. In your computer, stow your kit in the folder you use for your book. Later, when you have dozens of versions of a release, you may want to pack them into a dedicated media release folder or subfolder.

Many are convinced, usually based on stories they've heard rather than experienced, that your kit should be tricked up with gifts. Don't believe it. Plan the presentation of your kit to meet your branding goals, to sell your ideas to the media, and to help those editors and reviewers who have honored you with their interest do their work more easily.

Since the payola scandal of the 60s, many editors must refuse gifts. For that reason it is best to send a modest thank you gift a few days *after* the reporter or producer's work has been printed or aired. Trust me. These editors have enough fancy paper clips, magnets and pens. See chapter14 for creative gift and promotion items.

> Caveat: A kit left in an expo or tradeshow press room must compete with dozens of others. In this instance it attracts attention by sheer force of its design or because it includes a freebie. Editors must be gently coaxed to pick it up and tote it around the show with them. I believe that the best value-added gift you can include

is your book. Some new authors worry that an editor who can't possibly use the information in their kit will benefit but editors are VIPs in the publishing industry— they may pass their knowledge and interest on to others.

Chapter 4: Build Credentials For Your Kit

Publicity is like skipping a pebble across a puddle. You ll need to wind up and use your best form for that first pitch but sooner or later the ripples your effort produces are effortless.

CHJ: from an article for
ww.SellWritingOnline.com

Your credentials may already be impressive, but if this is your first book or if this book doesn't use expertise you gained in a present or past vocation, you'll need to build new "writerly" qualifications. There is no time like the present. The process is much like the one you experienced when you started your first job; you build a little at a time, one block at a time and soon, Voila! You have a castle.

One of the reasons you are structuring your media kit now is so you can easily see where your credentials need bolstering. Also, the very *process* of building credentials is a networking and publicity journey. Each success provides an opportunity for you to send out a release. Each release helps you foster contacts in the media and each experience adds luster to your publicity skills.

There are many building blocks available for constructing a literary edifice. In this chapter I suggest a few to build a sturdy foundation now, before your book is published. Later, in section III, you'll find others that are better used once you're holding your book in your hands.

Speaking: The Star of PR Campaigns

Speech and silence. We feel safer with a madman who talks than with one who cannot open his mouth.

E. M. Cioran, Rumanian-French Philosopher

Publicists dream about working with a client who can speak or is at least willing to learn. If you are frightened, let the birth of your book nudge you toward learning this skill. If after giving speech-making an honest effort, you decide not to actually give formal speeches, all your other appearances—from book signings to leading critique groups—will benefit your new speaking skills.

If you think of speaking as sharing, you may find that it fits your personality as well as a pair of comfy slippers. There are techniques that make being in front of a crowd less formal. As an example, at your launch you can take your microphone to the edge of the stage, sit down and talk as if you were speaking one-on-one with those who have come to wish you well. At a seminar you can use a mike with a long cord so you can go into the audience to answer questions—a casual and effective way to touch those who have come to see you. Beginning actors learn to minimize their fear of performing before others by holding a paper clip and focusing their attention on it instead of on the crowd. If you've ever taught or conducted meetings you are only extending those skills. Here are some ways to share information easily:

- Give handouts crammed with valuable information to members of theaudience, preferably something they'll keep. Print your pitch, the picture of your book cover and your contact information on each sheet.
- Use an old-fashioned notebook—the giant kind that fits on an easel. Write as you talk as if you were taking notes in your senior English class. You can use this technique as a cheat sheet by doing an outline before your presentation starts and filling in the secondary categories as you speak.
- Breathe deeply before you start speaking and have a glass of water on hand. If you've also provided munchies for the audience, the entire situation will feel more comfortable for you.

To unearth speaking engagements, watch the calendar sections in weekly and daily newspapers for coming events and locate entertainment agencies and organizations related to the topics you speak on in your yellow pages. Write a professional letter similar to a query and mail it to each lead. If you have a promotion gift or bookmark send one along with your letter. Wait a couple of weeks and then call to ask if they received your letter and follow up with a verbal pitch. Here are some other sources for finding places to speak:

- Fraternities and sororities.
- Night clubs and coffee houses.
- Corporations.
- Professional organizations.
- Charitable organizations.
- Political groups.
- Reading clubs.
- Libraries.
- Schools, especially college classes that are associated with some aspect of your book.

You can also propel one speech into others. In your handouts, include a form that asks the audience to recommend another organization that might benefit from your presentation. It will be more effective if you:

- Request that they turn the form back to you by the end of meeting.
- Design it as a self-mailer with pre-paid postage so they can send it later.
- Define the information you will need by using blanks for the name of the organization, kinds of programs preferred, officer in charge of programs, her phone number and e-mail.
- Offer a discount or perk with an expiration date.
- Offer your service at a reduced rate or at no charge to charitable events.

You may choose to charge for speaking. Occasionally an organization will offer only an honorarium. Sometimes I'll not charge a fee if the crowd is large enough and they will let me display and sell my book. I always ask the person in charge of programming if they'll mention my presentation in their newsletter and releases and include a picture of my book cover.

> Hint #1: Before the spotlight is trained on you, read FIRST IMPRESSIONS: WHAT YOU DON'T KNOW ABOUT HOW OTHERS SEE YOU by Ann Demarai and Valerie White.

> Hint #2: Improve your skills: Join Toastmasters Club. Take a basic speech class.

> Hint #3: Sign up for Tom Antion's newsletter to glean tips for polishing your verbal presentation. Email: tom@antion.com.

Hint #4: If you decide to charge for your service, $75 per hour with a two hour minimum is standard. Some accept fees from charities and then give it back as a donation.

Literary Contests

She whom I love is hard to catch and conquer, Hard, but O the glory of the winning were she won.
George Meredith

A contest is as a contest does. They are much more than a prize. They may appear at your door accompanied by money, an offer to publish your work, prestige or all three. Winning any contest—even placing as a finalist—is an opportunity for publicity.

Many pages have been written about contests in writers' periodicals. The article in POETRY AND WRITERS' Nov/Dec 2003 issue addresses some problems inherent in contests: For example, writers consider them rigged and resent the fees (usually from $10 to $25). Publishers and organizations become dependent on the fees they charge. Rarely does an unknown author win which is the whole point of many contests—to find delicious new voices that will keep the not-so-voracious appetite of publishers for new material well fed.

Many of the most reputable contests have fallen into one of these pitfalls or another and I believe you should not let that keep you from using this road to stardom. If you prefer, you can find no-fee contests. Some contests only accept nominations from publishers so yours may enter your book and pay the fee. You may need to prod your publisher a bit if you know of a contest for which you think your book would be suitable.

In terms of promotion, however, there is little that editors find more enticing than a winner—any winner. Here are some guidelines for using contests to gain exposure and expand your credentials:
- Set a goal based on the kind of writing you do and the size of your pocketbook. No-fee contests work well until you refine your contest IQ. Some journals award prizes to the best work submitted for their pages in a given year. Pick contests that impose fees at least as carefully as you might select a tomato from the produce department at your market.

- Find contests from a source that lists less popular contests as well as those that carry names like Hemingway and Faulkner.
- Choose contests that match your needs. Most first-time authors should submit their work for some small awards as well as large ones.
- Pay attention to the contest's guidelines. Don't enter a competition that seeks experimental fiction if your book is a mystery. It wastes your time and theirs even if no fee is involved.
- To increase your chances and to keep you from worrying about each entry, submit work to several contests at a time. Other tips for contest entries include:
  - Track entries so that you don't submit the same material to the same contest twice.
  - Ignore the insistence of some editors that you shouldn't submit simultaneously. This is patently unfair to the author.
  - Notify those you may have submitted to if your piece wins elsewhere.
  - Don't recycle copies from one contest to another. Editors complain about entries that look as if they have spent a night in the rain.

Find suitable contests on the Web, in books and through organizations. Here are a few:
- EPIC is an organization for authors of e-books but print authors may join. Their Eppies Award is gaining more prestige each year. Learn more at http://www.epicauthors.org/joinepic.html
- Use the "Deadlines" section of POETRY & WRITERS to find reputable contests. Most are very competitive and charge fees. Check them out at: www.pw.org
- CRWROPPS is an announcement list for contests and calls for submissions. To subscribe send an e-mail to crwropps-subscribe@topica.com.
- A fat volume called WRITER'S MARKETS publishes an updated edition each year. It is a valuable resource for more than contests. Because it costs about $40, you may want to borrow it from your library.
- www.Writer2writer.com includes a list of no-fee contests in most issues. To subscribe to their newsletter, send a blank e-mail to writertowriter-subscribe@yahoogroups.com.au.

- Connie Gotsch, author of A MOUTH FULL OF SHELL (http://www.authorsden.com/conniegotsch), won two awards from professional organizations, both national and regional. Check out your local Press Women, the National Federation of Press Women (http://www.nfpw.org/) and other organizations for details.
- Do a Google search on "writing contests" + your genre.

Once you've won a contest—finalist or first place—you are newsworthy:

- Add this honor to the "Awards" page of your media kit. If it's your first award, center it on a page of its own. Oh! And celebrate!
- Write your media release announcing this coup (see chapters 16 on composing a targeted media list and chapter three on writing releases).
- Post the release on press sites that allow you to post them yourself. Examples are www.zinos.com and www.prnews.com.
- Notify your professional (writing and other) organizations.
- Notify bookstores where you hope to have a signing and, later, those where you have had a signing.
- Most colleges have press offices. If they do, put the administrator on your media list and make an effort to meet her. Ditto for the editors of your school/college periodicals.
- Add this information to the signature feature (see chapter six) of your e-mail program.
- Add this honor to the template you will use in future media releases—the part that gives an editor background on you.
- Use this information when you pitch TV or radio producers. It sets you apart from other others and defines you as an expert.

> Hint: If your book wins a contest that doesn't provide labels, have some made to apply to the cover of your book a la the famous Caldecott award. Don't forget to notify your publisher!

Your other Writing

> If my doctor told me I had only six minutes to live, I wouldnt brood. Id type a little faster.
> Isaac Asimov

Writing is what we do! How wonderful it is that we can promote our book by writing. Here are some possibilities:

Write and Recycle Articles

Collect some of your old writing. Rewrite sections of your book as excerpts. Put on your big idea sombrero and think of articles that will appeal to your readers. Then find a publisher to showcase them. Or you can do it the other way around. Find publishers who appeal to the reader you want to reach and write an article for them.

When I began to think about promoting my book, I had scraps of my writing secreted away in the nooks and crannies of my computer like little emerald-cut diamonds in the dark recesses of a safe. What good were they doing hidden away like that? Some had been submitted and rejected and some had been ignored altogether. That made them equal because regardless of the reason, no one had read them! There were even a few that had been printed—some on obscure websites that had purchased first-time rights only and these cried out to be read again.

Then I noticed new literary journals sprouting up everywhere. Brand new print and Web journals edited by people who care about literature even though they may not pay a cent. I began a rescue mission. I retrieved a few stories and poems from my files, submitted them and some were published.

> Caveat: Sites that print previously published material should credit the first publisher.

Many cringe at the idea of submitting material without an expectation of financial compensation. However, it is a time-honored tradition among poets and literary writers to publish gratis. Further, people have bartered for eons and considered it fair and just. If your article is published with a tagline, complete with URL for your site on the Web, it will help your branding efforts, expose your book and boost your search engine ranking. That's because these engines send spiders that reach into webland to find material and they put a high value on sites with frequent links. That's why it is so important to include your website address on anything you submit to the Web.

In order to encourage you, I'm listing print and electronic publishers that used some of my work in just 30 days or so after I began my recycling campaign. The list may reassure some of you—especially those who have not yet found a publisher—that your voice is worth listening to and illustrate that even an article once rejected by the ATLANTIC REVIEW (that, mind you, gets something like 30,000 submissions a year!) might bring readers pleasure and serve as a promotion tool. If any of these publications suit the material you have closeted away, edit and submit! That may be all it takes to turn you from a literary couch potato into a spirited PR genius:

- TheCopperfieldReview.com published both a poem and an excerpt from my novel, www.copperfieldreview.com.
- The Banyan Review, www.banyanreview.com.
- SubtleTea, www.subtletea.com.
- Sparks Magazine, print, www.sparksmagazine.com.
- Penumbra, California State University at Stanislaus' annual literary journal, print.
- The Feminist Journal, www.thefeministjournal.com.
- Poetic Voices, www.PoeticVoices.com.
- The Yarrow Brook Review Journal, print, published both a poem and a short story. Now the editor publishes only online at www.wordthunder.com.
- Long Story Short http://quicksitebuilder.cnet.com/mywritingfriend/id203.html.

I should mention that not one of these reimbursed me with anything but a thank you, a lovely link, byline and tagline. A writer must choose her goals. I chose to share and expose my work.

Another author who understands the value of giving material away is Jodi Helmer, a freelancer and editor based in Portland (http://jodihelmer.com). Because she agreed to write for a very small fee, she was offered a freelance job at $1.00 a word (considered good freelance pay). Exposure, whether for free or for low pay is often worth much more than the paycheck itself.

When you personally contact editors you widen your contacts in the writing community but you can also find publishers by using article banks and where publishers go to find professional content. Here are leads to some of those places:

- You'll find a list of both kinds of opportunities at www.bellaonline.com/articles/art3219.asp.

- When you post articles on these banks, include URLs for your website, for your picture, for your book cover and a mini biography that mentions your book (s) and, if you have one, your autoresponder e-mail address.
- An example of a portal (another word for article banks) is www.PowerHomeBiz.com. It uses only business articles. Here are some others:
  - www.Articles123.com.
  - www.netterweb.com/articles.
  - www.allnetarticles.com.
  - www.womans-net.com.
  - www.ezine-writer.com.au.
  - www.clickforcontent.com.
  - www.freezinesite.com.
  - www.IdeaMarketers.com.
  - www.family-content.com.
  - www.ezine-writer.com/article-lists.html.
  - www.ezine-writer.com/top10.html.
  - www.writers.net.
  - Phantom Writers Article Distribution Service is an article bank that reaches more than 6000 publishers and webmasters with free reprint articles. Go to: http://thePhantomWriters.com.

For updates on publishers that will publish your work try:
- This site, http://www.writingcorner.com/admin/sub-guidelines.htm, is a good source for publishers looking for content.
- Kimberly Ripley puts out a newsletter called FREELANCING LATER IN LIFE http://writerippublishing.c.topica.commaabTuUaa5Bbpa2Q6Deb/. In it she always shares a source list and writing tips.
- Fran Silverman's bi-weekly BOOK PROMOTION NEWSLETTER for writers of all genres is well worth her $5 fee. Send an e-mail to franalive@optonline.net. You'll learn lots about marketing a book. You also can submit articles about book promotion to her, for soon you will be an expert on at least one aspect of this subject. Learn more at: www.bookpromotionnewsletter.com.
- Another helpful site is http://www.theroseandthornezine.com. Sign up for their newsletter that lists markets.

> Caveat: Do not post or offer any article in trade that you may want to sell later. Many journals buy only first rights; if your piece has appeared on the Web it will not qualify under most publishers' guidelines.

In their excellent newsletter, SPAN CONNECTION, Small Publishers Association of North America suggests a useful site that will help you place your work before those who are most likely to read your book. Www.ranks.com lists sites by category. If you've written a cookbook, you search for matches to key words like "health," "nutrition," and "cooking" A romance novelist might choose words like "Regency," "romance," "historical," and "erotic." You figure out the categories because you're the one who knows your book and your reader best.

Here are some tips that will help you get more promotional mileage out of your articles regardless of how you choose to disseminate them:

- Include information about your book in the article itself if you can figure out how to make that information pertinent to the article. Editors who use free material won't mind a little self-promotion if it isn't blatant.
- Submit a resource box or sidebar (those helpful little informationals that are sometimes surrounded by a border; they often appear with feature articles on the Web and in print). Include your own book on the list. Resource boxes are added value for the editor and a few who pay for their articles will pay more for a thoughtfully-written one.
- Invite editors to visit your website in search of free material and to sign up for your notices about available articles. Capture their information and categorize it so you can better serve them in the future. A drop-down form that includes the subjects you write about is a handy way to make sure you provide what they want.
- Don't date your articles with limiting content. Use "recently," instead of a specific date. Ditto for copyrights. The copyright insignia and your name is enough.
- A program like SpamAssassin assures your editors that the content in your article will not bounce their newsletters. Add a note to each contribution that says, "This article was checked by (whatever program you used)." Keep a list of editors who used your material or might need it.

(See the section on "syndicating" later in this chapter for information on how to use these names.)

> Hint #1: If you use an autoresponder, your editors can request an article and it will be sent back to them automatically. Www.sendfree.com is a user-friendly one. You can't track requests as well as if you handle them yourself, but autoresponders are time-savers.

> Hint #2. Wherever you stow your articles, use plain text files. Your editors will be grateful for material that has not been garbled by cyberspace.

> Hint #3: For more in-depth information on writing and selling articles read Vicki Hinze's ALL ABOUT WRITING TO SELL: A BESTSELLING WRITER TO WRITER'S GUIDE TO THE CRAFT, BUSINESS AND SECRETS OF GETTING PUBLISHED in 3.5 diskette. Find it at Amazon.com.

> Hint #4: Submit your article with a title. Type in the byline exactly as you would like to see it. Example: "By Marlena Thompson, author of A RARE & DEADLY ISSUE. Include a short tagline (see chapter two); don't expect your editor to do it for you.

Write a Column

A logical way to land a regular column of your own is to examine the articles you've written, identify a media trend and parlay select few with a specific theme into a proposal. They will become the basis—your clippings—for convincing an editor of your expertise. Now all you need to do is come up with an appropriate column name and enough courage to approach the right editor.

When my husband and I closed our last retail shop, I took old, yellowed clips from writing I had done in the 1950s into THE PASADENA STAR NEWS. Nothing ventured, nothing gained, I thought. Still, I was sure the features editor would politely show me to the door. Perhaps because I was so brazen, the editor immediately assigned me a column called "Savvy Shopper" for that newspaper and its affiliates that I wrote for several years.

Don't assume that whatever samples you have aren't enough. It's better if you can offer two or three published articles that have the same theme but one may do if your theme is strong. That an article has been published gives you credibility, but you might present only a sample column you have written as well. If you have written frequent op-ed pieces or letters-to-the editor they may be an entrée to your own column.

Once you have experience of any kind, an editor may be willing to take a chance on something with a different slant. According to Charlotte Degregorio (cvpress@yahoo.com), editors are looking for information that will be useful to their readers but they also need responsible writers who write well and submit on time. In her STANDARD PERIODICAL DIRECTORY, she categorizes entries that make it easy for you to find an editor who might be interested in your work.

Once you're accepted as a columnist, sell only the first rights. The new columns you will be writing may then be recycled at a later date. The reverse is also true; occasions will arise when you can use material you've gathered in the past for your new column.

> Hint: Ask for free tips on this subject by sending an SASE (Self Addressed Stamped Envelope) to: Charlotte Digregorio, author of YOU CAN BE A COLUMNIST, Civetta Press, PO Box 1043 Portland OR 97207.

Syndicate Your Column

Once you have credentials and a reference, consider syndication. Imagine how much better books would sell for a nationally known columnist like Liz Smith or Andy Rooney than for someone who is not known by the public.

Once you have a track record, you might submit a proposal to small services or large ones like the Associated Press (AP). Do a search on "syndicates" for ideas. You'll want to know what kinds of columns they already have, where yours might fit in, and the appropriate editors' name.

One author, Paul St. John Fleming turned the table around. He propelled his columns and life as a benevolent copper that he wrote for THE SALT LAKE TRIBUNE into a book called BETWEEN DONUTS.

Self -Syndicate Your Column

There are two ways to self-syndicate. You can bypass syndicates to sell your own columns to different outlets yourself—one at a time until you start getting famous. Or you can give your articles away, syndication style. The latter is really only an efficient way to recycle the essays, columns, commentaries and rants you have written. I have organized this process to meet my needs; I have no idea if anyone else does it similarly, but it disseminates writing widely and quickly.

> Caveat: This system only works if you are writing for publicity only and not selling your material. To make it work for true self-syndication, the system would need to be adapted only slightly

My approach is very informal. I send articles I write on how authors can get "free" ink to one group of editors, my pieces on tolerance to another and so on. I keep the addresses of all the editors I know who don't require exclusive material in a "Note" in my Outlook program or in the address book of my e-mail program. When I have written an opinion piece, review, rant or whatever, I open the note feature of Outlook for a particular group of editors, copy and paste their addresses into an e-mail address window. The next steps are:

- Think of a clear and catchy subject line.
- Be sure that each e-mail address in the window is "blind," that is, it should have parentheses around it and a comma between the addresses. That way your query-submission looks more personal.
- Include a signature line with complete contact information—website, e-mail address, and phone number.
- It is unorthodox but I paste my article or review into the e-mail and introduce it with a query that is generic enough to work for any editor who receives it. By doing so, I save a step and the editors on my list all know me. In the query I make these points:
  - That the article is free.
  - That I would like the editor to use the piece in its entirety and include the byline and tagline as submitted. Clearly delineating your expectations is not demanding; it is professional.
  - That when the article appears I would like notification including the web address.

> Caveat: Do not attach your article. Many virus-wary editors (and others) will not open an e-mail or its attachment if one is included.

- Double check for typos (which, I'm not happy to tell you I sometimes miss).
- Sometimes, I offer an editor an exclusive, especially if I can parlay it into extra exposure by gently asking for more than a byline and tagline.
- Among those who might be included on the list are:
  - Newsletter editors—even authors with their own newsletters—use book reviews, articles about writing, tips and more.
  - Columnists.
  - Website coordinators.
  - Editors of every ilk.

> Hint: You may prefer to sell your work before you give it away in return for exposure. If so, sign away only first rights. Then follow the guidelines above for recycling these previously published pieces to other publications—within the terms of the first contract, of course.

List Yourself in Wikipedia

In terms of time, authors are experienced waiters. Even if we never waited tables while we were anticipating our big break, most of us learned to loiter patiently by the sidelines. Authors who appear to be overnight successes generally have done their share of dallying in the shadow of others. It's just that no one talks about it. Overnight success is much more newsworthy.

So here I am, flipping through the pages of TIME MAGAZINE and there it is. A chance to be listed in an encyclopedia right up there with Marcel Proust and Chekhov—with no waiting necessary! This article in TIME wasn't directed at authors and it doesn't suggest that anyone who longs for fame gets it instantly by adding her name to what this news magazine's editors call The People's Encyclopedia. But what a fun opportunity for writers! Go to http://wikipedia.org to add an entry, correct an entry or, lo! Create a new entry. There are plenty of help links to guide you along. I am no tekky and I was able to figure out how to do it.

The title, "Wiki" comes from the Hawaiian word for "fast." I presume this is because a very speedy way to put together an encyclopedia is to let others do it for you—at the speed of net which is darn near as fast as the speed of light.

Because so many authors are modest—some would argue suppressed is a better word—you may think that you or your book will be immediately edited out. That is not the way this is supposed to work. Of course someone else might come along and edit your material, but the risk of being disparaged isn't any greater than having your book available for sale (and therefore available for review) on Amazon. Of course, this process is an inducement not to exaggerate your literary importance. That seems highly unlikely because most authors are downright self-effacing. Still, it would be nice to realize a dream right here and now. So have at it.

Wikipedia is a free, nonprofit site that has 150,000 encyclopedia-style entries. I did it just for the fun of it! Do a search on my name or on THIS IS THE PLACE to see what comes up. You'll notice there are a couple of typos. Being tech-illiterate, I couldn't figure out how to fix them. I'm sure you'll do better.

You can also post one of those articles I've been encouraging you to write for exposure. Don't forget to include your website URL and your ISBN (if you have one) in your tagline.

> Caveat: I have no idea whether this sells books or not. It is fun, free and may offer possibilities I've not yet conceived. That makes it a better use of time than playing computer solitaire.

Publish Your Own Newsletter
Some authors find sending out a newsletter to their readers—fans if you will—an excellent way to promote sales of their book and to keep readers interested for the next and the next. It isn't for everyone; I opted for frequent exposure (media release, articles, columns and book and movie reviews) in newsletters written by others. I make e-friends that way; editors appreciate my contributions and I reach beyond my own base of readers.

Linda Morelli (romriter@aol.com) swears by her newsletter. The author of FIERY SURRENDER, Linda says, "I have more fun with my quarterly newsletters (than other forms of promotion). I personalize each with news about what's happening in my world, my latest reviews and book signings, my current contest, and even my favorite recipes." Although she sends out about 100 letters by USPS to fans who don't "do" e-mail, she posts electronically to a much larger list. Go to this link http://members.aol.com/lbmwriter/romance/Newsletter.htm or e-mail Linda for a sample of one of her letters. She will be grateful for—you guessed it—the exposure.

It may be easier for romance writers like Linda to fill their letters with material that will be of interest to their readers but it can be done for any genre. Here are some tips on how you might start:

- Keep your goals in mind. Entertainment? Staying in contact with readers? Garnering support? Book sales?
- Decide on the frequency of your letter depending on the amount of time and money you want to give over to it if you choose to do a snail mail edition. Also consider the time involved in editing it. Factor in the time you will need for your other promotion efforts.
- Most letters start with a chatty piece from the author. The author disseminates news about her book, the writing she is doing elsewhere and more. If she uses people's names in this section it will be read more thoroughly than if the letter is "me" centered. Humor will also get and keep readers.
- Let people on your list contribute articles. That increases readership.
- Include a letters-to-the-editor section. Your readers will want to participate and will be more likely to open their mail if they think their name might appear in your letter.
- Include general and fun features to entertain your readers. A crossword puzzle, anyone?
- Ask your readers for suggestions on content they would like to see included.
- Post each newsletter on your website.
- Use a window so that visitors to your site can sign up to receive your letter. Some of your regular subscribers will revisit your archived letters and sites if you have included a feature that is useful to them.

> Caveat: If you send out a letter that's geared only to other authors, it won't help you promote your books beyond a certain audience.

Hint #1: Be sure to announce your events.

Hint #2: Suggest that your readers call in with questions to radio programs, chat rooms or wherever else you appear. When your writing is featured on a website, ask them to comment in the site's guestbook. When it appears in a print, urge them to write a letter-to-the-editor. Your readers will love sharing the spotlight with you.

Write Reviews

Why not? You read anyway. Reading contributes to the quality of your own writing. It takes less time to write a review than to read a book. It exposes your name via bylines and taglines to a most important audience—people who read books. Perhaps, after they've read your reviews, they'll read *your* book.

Mary Gannon, a deputy editor of POETS & WRITERS MAGAZINE, says that reviewers take "a lot of heat…for some free books, a few bucks and a byline." However, it's usually only the most famous reviewers—those who review for THE NEW YORK TIMES BOOK REVIEW, as an example—who are disparaged for their criticism and only the radical or caustic ones at that.

I overcame my fear of reviewing someone else's book by deciding that, if I couldn't recommend the book I was reading, I wouldn't write a review. I started slowly and before long I had a whole list of book sites clamoring for reviews, editors who were happy to use my byline, tagline, website link, sometimes even a picture of my book cover—all in trade for reviews.

As an author-reviewer, yours is not to make enemies but rather to:
- Give honest feedback to the authors of the books you review as well as to your readers. Authors can learn much from well-meant criticism.
- Get bylines and taglines that tell about you, your expertise and your book (see chapter two and the index entries for uses of taglines).
- Get paid for your reviews, though for the purpose of THE FRUGAL BOOK PROMOTER, I'm assuming that you

will be doing them for no charge, basically trading them for exposure.

- Place your reviews where they will be read frequently.
- Recycle your reviews, that is, place them where you retain all rights (see the section on recycling and syndicating articles in this chapter).
- Build relationships with editors and fellow reviewers. Such relationships make it easier for you to obtain a review of your own book when it is released.

> Caveat: Reviewing can take on a life of its own. Set limits early on or it will leave you little time for your other writing.

The how-tos of actually writing a review are not in the purview of this book. I chose a critique style that is comfortable for me and then found publishers with similar guidelines. I then fine-tuned my reviews to accommodate the needs of sites with large readership.

> Caveat: Consider that the long, essay-type reviews used in the book sections of newspapers are more time-consuming than short ones composed to grab a Web visitor's attention. It is also much easier to find Web editors that will accept content from new people.

Web reviews give you what Jacqueline Lichtenberg calls a "footprint" on the search engines. That is a valuable presence in the eyes of producers and editors who may be searching for an expert on a certain topic or, even just checking up on you for a possible profile or interview. I was one of several authors who participated in a recent Literacy Day campaign, but I was the one who ended up on ABC TV's nightly news because of that footprint.

Whether you are compensated with cash or with exposure for your book, your reviews will be good writing samples and publishing credentials in the future. Here are a few sites to try:

- www.bookreviewcafe.com uses short, professionally written reviews.
- www.rebeccasreads.com gives very specific guidelines for her reviews.
- www.myshelf.com sometimes looks for reviewers who will offer them exclusives.

- www.simegen.com runs a reviews section.
- www.thebookportal.co.uk/contribute.asp. Send your reviews in plain text file.
- http://www.bookreviewcorner.com/authidx.php.

> Hint: I developed a type of review that I consider to be original, if there is such a thing in the world. I assess a famous writer's work as if she had submitted it to critique group. I look for writing techniques she uses superbly or not so well, ones that emerging authors can emulate—or not. It's a cross between a how-to article and a review. I found editors of sites that cater to the needs of writers enthusiastic about them. You might build such a niche with your own idea.

Write for Anthologies

Let anthologies publicize for you. It's easy. Watch for calls for submissions, then write something or send something you've already written that matches the publication's needs. Sometimes they'll pay you for it, sometimes not. No matter. Your name and your book will receive exposure with an added measure of credibility because you are published within its covers; often you will receive much more than you gave.

Some authors do not feel that anthologies work well because the pay is often little or nonexistent; they feel they are exploited because they are "expected" to buy the book and to promote it. As a starter, expectations are different from contractual agreements. Further, you would probably want to buy a couple of books to give to special people in your life and to editors who may then give you (and the anthology) some publicity. These pundits overlook the fact that many of our nation's finest review journals and anthologies do not pay their authors and that these publications are accepted entrées into the upper echelons of the literary world.

Because she knew my work had been published in several anthologies, Mary Emma Allen (me.allen@juno.com) interviewed me for a column she writes called "Promoting Your Prose." She told me, "Lately there has been much controversy about anthologies and some writers feel they're being taken advantage of when they contribute. I've never felt this way and, as long as I knew the rules up front, have enjoyed being published in them."

Some of what you see in this chapter is taken directly from that interview with Mary Emma. So, not so incidentally, this section of THE FRUGAL BOOK PROMOTER is an example of recycled writing that this chapter suggests as a tool for promotion. Those of us who hardly ever use their delete buttons later find a use for what we left behind as only computer clutter. A benefit of recycling is that a writer who recycles her work may feel less resentful about not being paid. Another is that recycling saves time.

My first "anthology" was a group effort e-book. Promotion-savvy authors were invited to contribute; we all knew that our participation would be only as successful as the total of each participant's promotional efforts. We were to give our e-book away rather than sell it. This is a good example a cross-promotion. We began to share our promotional coups using an e-group on Yahoogroups.com, became friends, joined one another in other projects, supported one another. Where is the exploitation in that? The process worked so well, I began to consider anthologies published by traditional publishers, university presses and others.

Anthologies sometimes pay their authors and almost always credit them with a tagline or other acknowledgement. Here are some other advantages:
- Anthologies may offer the chance at an award. One of my stories appeared in an unpaid anthology but it also carried with it the "Red Sky Press Award." Awards, especially ones chosen by prestigious judges like Rose A. O. Kleidon, Professor Emeritus in English at the University of Akron, can be used to promote in dozens of different ways. For ways to use awards, see the index. For information on garnering awards see chapter four under literary contests. To research this award go to http://www.bookmasters.com/kleidon/passfail.htm.
- Anthology editors may set up group book signing to promote the collection. My critique group partner, JayCe Crawford (www.authorsden.com/jaycecrawford) will be signing in LA for the A CUP OF COMFORT series in which her story "Being There" appears. Other anthologies include GOD ALLOWS U TURNS, CHOCOLATE FOR A WOMAN'S SOUL and the CHICKEN SOUP series. Anthology editors should not object to your passing out your author cards or book marks that promote your own book at their events. In addition, after you've participated,

you'll have a personal contact with an events coordinator at a major book store.

- The release of an anthology, book signings for anthologies or any other related events or awards are opportunities for an author to send out her own media releases; this is not just exposure, it's credible exposure.
- Some anthologies give a portion or all of their net profit to a selected charity.
- You may meet someone in the publishing world from whom you can learn new things or people who will introduce you to others with similar interests. Hooray for networking!

Authors concerned about being taken advantage of, should certainly be cautious. But they shouldn't reject an opportunity of being read and maybe even "discovered" based on someone else's bad experience or paranoia. I urge authors not to adopt the attitudes of others but to evaluate each offer individually, to hold each opportunity up to the light of her own career goals and her own standards. Publicity should be an adventure but it should also be ethical. We must listen to our own inner voices.

Write Introductions
I was asked to write an introduction for a book last year. I had no idea of the benefits of doing so, but it sounded fun. Eric Dinyer, is an artist who had a concept for a gift book called EFFORT AND SURRENDER: THE ART AND WISDOM OF YOGA. I have been thrilled with the results. Andrews McMeel Publishing used my name on the cover—nearly as prominently as the author's. I'm sure that Eric had something to do with that, but no matter. It is a product I am pleased to be associated with; that makes this project a perfect addition to my branding campaign. It occurs to me that an author might pursue introductions by letting it be known they are open to this kind of activity when they network with other writers and artists.

Write a Tip Sheet
A tip sheet is the way to editors' hearts. It is a list of quick, readable entries that relate to a specific subject. Editors often use one or more tips to fill nooks and crannies in their layouts. They also know that their readers love them. The subject line "Tip Sheet" is the most welcome message in any editor's e-mail box.

It is true that fiction writers must tweeze their material to make PR techniques like this work but the results are well worth the effort. Nonfiction writers will likely find tip sheets come popping off the pages of their book for them. Here are some ideas:

- List events in a "time-line." This is ideal for the writers of history, regency and other period romances or historical novels.
- Do a list of interesting statistics that deal with an aspect of your book. You might emulate TIME MAGAZINE's "Numbers" column.
- The publicity firm I once worked for instituted The Ten Best Dressed List. This was a publicity coup that built more than one career. Do a "best" or "worst" list that relates to something in your book. I do "Carolyn's Noble Prize List" of little known literary prose as opposed to Nobel's prize that almost always goes to artists who are already stars. My list is published annually in my "Back to Literature" column for MyShelf.com and I rewrite it to use as an Amazon.com "So You'd Like to…Guide" about six months after it is first published.
- Editors like "Top 5" or "Top 10" lists. These lists adapt themselves to how-to books.
- Lists of "the unusual" are good. I used one about Utah's idiosyncrasies to intrigue radio show hosts. When THIS IS THE PLACE was released. I worded such a list in a "Did you know" format. "Did you know that residents of Utah consume more catsup per capita than any other state in the union?"
- TIME MAGAZINE uses a list of quotes in a column called "Verbatim" each week. This might work especially well for a literary writer with a targeted media list.
- I may use this very list on writing tip sheets that you are reading to market THE FRUGAL BOOK PROMOTER. It could be published on sites where authors congregate. I would hope it would entice authors to want to read the whole book.

> Hint: For tip sheet ideas go to http://Top7business.com. Each day it features one new list of seven ways to solve a problem; their archives are equally valuable. You might submit a suitable tip list to this site for publication. Include your photo, your tagline and your contact information.

Here is an example of a tip sheet, though, I would probably need to delete the bulleted portion if I were to submit it to a publisher. They are for your eyes only.

Ten Great Ways to Prepare for the Big Day

1. Learn to write a memorable query letter. A query letter is your sharpest selling instrument.
   - Check out WRITER'S MARKET at the library; you'll find a good how-to section in the front of every edition.
   - Purchase Marc Sadowski's pamphlet that covers query letters and other important topics at: http://www.bookink.com/publishing_advice.html.
   - Read real query letters that landed freelance assignments that paid over $2,000 at http://www.writersweekly.com/books/1409.html. Adapt them to your own needs.
2. Learn more about promotion and writing. While you're doing it, build a list of ideas for future marketing. Here are some places to start:
   - http://csfwg.org/resources.htm will lead you to many more resources.
   - http://quicksitebuilder.cnet.com/mywritingfriend/ Long Short Story publishes articles, poetry, short fiction and offers critiques.
   - http://www.apolloslyre.com This site is open to queries for writing or promotion oriented articles, poetry, reviews and fiction.
3. Start a list of local book stores and libraries.
4. Build a list of retail outlets other than bookshops that might carry your book. You'll find such a list especially useful if you write nonfiction.
5. Check E-bay and learn the ropes for selling your book there.
6. Attend seminars on publishing and writing at book fairs and art expos. The Small Publishers Association of North America's fall conference and trade show is especially good. Call (719) 395-4790 for information

7. Take a class in Word or Web skills.
8. Better your presentation skills by taking a class in storytelling. Go to Doug Stevenson's site, www.storytheater.net.
9. Learn about the publishing world including subsidy publishing and self-publishing. Publishing is your business now. You need to understand all sides of it. Here is one of my Amazon Listmanias with some title suggestions:http://www.amazon.com/exec/obidos/tg/listmania/list-browse/-/2HMJ9JPRE7LXW/ref=cm_aya_av.lm_more/103-9758246-4851851.
10. Attend gift shows. Look for ideas for:
    - Articles.
    - Possible representatives or distributors for your book, especially how-to books or other nonfiction.
    - Promotion items.

Chapter 5: What You Can Learn At Writers' Conferences

A series of writers conferences may be the near-equivalent of an MFA for the time-starved writer juggling her creative aspirations and the requirements of her day job.

CHJ, from an article for
www.bookreviewcafe.com

Writers' conferences are valuable because they immerse an author—albeit for a few short days—into her art. They expose her to a broad array of what she needs for success, and make her aware of how much she must know to publish and promote. They allow her to sample a little of each or zealously immerse herself in one.

I once read an editorial at www.RebeccasReads.com by an author who was less than thrilled with a conference she had attended. She hoped to snag an agent or publisher. After her experience there, she threw up her hands in horror and decided to self-publish or subsidy-publish but she also berated conferences as worthless. I thought that she might be frustrated because:

- She attended the wrong conference at the wrong time in her sojourn from first draft to publishing.
- She set unrealistic goals for the conference.
- Her expectations for what a conference would provide were too narrow.

I am convinced anew of the need for conferences when, after an author's book is published, I hear her express surprise at how involved she must be in its promotion. It would be difficult to come away from a conference without developing a handle on what a book requires to make it visible.

I also worry that there are many unqualified or barely qualified people teaching writing, grammar, promotion and other subjects aimed at authors on the Web and elsewhere. An author may be assured that if she chooses a conference staged by a large university, writing school or well-known magazine she'll have a better chance of getting up-to-date, accurate advice.

Aside from the credibility of most conferences, here is what you'll miss if you never go to one:

- You'll miss a chance to learn about traditional and nontraditional publishing. If you aren't well-advised, you will doubt your own choices when things go awry (and a few things always go awry—it's the way of the world).
- You'll miss all those writing secrets that seminars offer. You can't hear a secret if you aren't in the room.
- You will miss out on contacts with more publishers, agents and marketers than you're likely to meet elsewhere in a decade.
- You'll miss the greatest possible critique partners. Conference-goers tend to be excellent critiquers because they cared enough to learn about their craft. If you don't already have *skilled* critique partners, forming a new group should be one of your goals for a conference.
- If you don't attend, your chance of corralling one of the reputable agents in attendance is a big fat 0. If you do go, your chances are slim but you at least have one! A good agent can also be a valuable editor and promotion partner. If she sees promise in your book she may help you mold it into a commercially viable entity.
- If you don't attend a conference, you'll miss the chance to practice your pitch and may never learn how a really good one works.
- If you don't attend a conference, you'll never know what you missed—both the good and the bad.

How to Choose a Conference

> I will not choose what many men desire,
> Because I will not jump with common spirits,
> And rank me with the barbarous multitudes.
> William Shakespeare

The Prince of Arragon in THE MERCHANT OF VENICE got it right. There are times when it pays to be picky. Selecting a writers' conference must be a made with much consideration given to the individual needs of the writer.

Determine your goals and choose a conference accordingly. Some are decidedly promotion oriented. Others tend to be entrées to agents and publishers. Some are places that will help you hone your writing skills; most will do a little of each.

- Study up on conferences. Get back issues of POETS & WRITERS that include articles—really reviews—of conferences. Use your connections to get both opinions and suggestions from writers who have attended.
- Do not choose a conference based on its exotic location unless your first interest is a vacation.
- If you choose a conference that offers critiques of your work by publishers or agents for an additional fee, spend the extra money to do this. If you wait until later, you may have to kick in another full conference fee for the privilege.
- If a face-to-face with an agent is what you are really after, wait to go to a conference until you are prepared to utilize this perk.

> Hint: If enticing an agent is your primary goal, know the agents who will be in attendance. Research their names on the net. Ask other authors about them. If none are suitable for your book, choose another conference. If you are determined to interview with a specific agent, sign up for the conference early enough to be assured of an audience with your choice.

Determine the thrust of the conference you will be attending. Because of proximity and prestige, UCLA (www.uclaextension.edu/writers) has access to Hollywood as a resource. This makes their "Studio" one of the best in the nation for screenwriters. Conferences located in remote areas may suit those who want to extend their visit for a writing retreat.

Watch the credentials of the conference teachers. If you write persona poems, you may want to study with a teacher who has had success in that specific kind of poetry like UCLAs Suzanne Lummis. A person who is interested in writing courtroom dramas will benefit from an author who has published in that genre.

Tips for Making the Most of a Conference:

> Treat a conference like a garden. Bring home all the ripe stuff you can find.
>
> CHJ

In order to get as much from a writers' conference as possible you will need to organize. This is your guide for doing just that. Without it you would not be able to glean the most from one—at least not until after you've already attended your first.

If you go with friends, copy this section of THE FRUGAL BOOK PROMOTER and encourage them to prepare in advance. Also split up. You'll learn more and make more contacts for your publishing and promotion goals; share them with one another later.

Your notebook is key to getting the most from a conference:

- Bring a seven-subject notebook. On each separator page tape a #10 envelope in which you can slip business cards, bookmarks, mini-notes to yourself, and small brochures. When you arrive home, part of your filing and sorting will be done.
- Divide the notebook into sections that match your goals for this conference. These might include: Agents, Publishers, Promotion, Writing, and Other Contacts. Leave one section to be assigned to a category that may crop up after you arrive.
- Take blank mailing labels to make index tabs that stick out from the edge of the notebook.

> Hint: Bring a small pouch—I use one I received with an Estée Lauder gift with purchase. Toss into it color coded pens, snub-nosed scissors (you may need to get them through airport security), a small roll of cellophane tape, your index labels, paperclips, strong see-through packing tape, hammer, tacks, razor, Chapstick, hole punch, breath mints, elastic bands, Band-Aids and your personal medication. Don't unpack this. You'll need it in the future.

At the back of your conference notebook make a directory section. Use the label index markers to delineate each one.

- The first page is a name and address list for publishers. They should be listed in conference handouts but you may glean more from seminars. Star the ones you spoke to and note something you learned about each: Make notes like what they publish that is similar to your book or if they made any suggestions to you—anything that will help them place you when you write to them and mention your encounter. Query letters work best when you indicate that you are familiar with the person or company being queried.

> Big Hint: When you talk to publishers always ask them what they do to promote their authors' books. Pin them down to specifics.

- The second page is for fellow authors. Extend your notes. It's no fun to arrive home with a useless business card.
- Ditto for agents. Another for conference planners. You may be surprised at how often you'll refer to this page.
- A page for "Other Resources" includes information on anything from other conferences to books you'd like to read.
- Designate a few pages for writing ideas.
- The final pages are for new promotion ideas.
- On the first night, of the conference, clip and paste separate parts of the conference handouts into your notebook.
- When you arrive home transfer essential contact information into your data base. Use codes and notes to nudge your memory later. The future will provide ways for you to keep in contact including inviting many to your book launch.

> Hint #1: Some conferences offer tables for participants to leave promotional handouts. Ask your conference coordinator how you might utilize this opportunity.

> Hint #2: Ask the conference coordinator if they publish a newsletter or journal. If so, send the editor media releases as your career moves along.

> Hint #3: Find other bona fide educational institutions that offer onsite and Web classes. Examples are Gotham Writers' Workshop in New York (http://writingclasses.com); and The Image Warehouse, Athens

Chapter 6: Use the Web

The most powerful tool a writer has today is the Internet.

Jacqueline Lichtenberg, sci-fi writer

In terms of promotion, the message is as simple as this: The opportunities the net offers are varied, easily researched and generally about as free as promotion opportunities get. Most of the ideas under the "Building Credentials" section of this book (see chapter four) may be used on the Web and, as you already know, they help your branding efforts in addition to providing fodder for your media kit.

Hint: Sarah Mankowski, author of LIBERATION, says when you post press releases or information about your books online, include your ISBN—the number on the back of your book near the barcode. Do as the online stores do—omit the hyphens. Once your book is published you can do a search on that number to see how well this trick has been working for you.

Your Own Website

It is impossible to beg editorial space or buy advertising space that is as targeted, available and useful as your own website.

CHJ

Commercially successful authors like Scott Turow (www.scottturow.com) have their own websites. Some like Nora Roberts (www.noraroberts.com) personalize their sites by writing its copy in first person. Publishers are both coaxing and commanding their authors to build a site. This is not an aspect of your promotion campaign that you can dismiss without risk.

If you are not technically adept enough to build a website or you haven't the time for it, hire it done or ask a computer savvy friend to design one for you in trade for a lifetime of gratitude. We're discussing it now to give you plenty of time to take classes, explore, and make mistakes.

When THIS IS THE PLACE was published, I decided to make life easy on myself and skip the HTML route altogether. Those initials are scary things for me. I found myself a webmaster and for $100 a year I get an address of my own at The Literary Times. It even has a guestbook, which I'd love you to sign. I don't think I ask my webmaster for too much (he may disagree) but it appears that his service is "unlimited" at one set price and I feel comfortable with that kind of financial arrangement. However, reality hit me soon after I enlisted my webmaster's help.

Hiring a webmaster does not absolve the author of responsibilities. Decide how much you want to spend for the care and feeding of a site and its master. If you hire a designer/webmaster to do a site for you and only for you, (a stand-alone domain of your own) it can be expensive. Instead, you can piggy back on another website that is a home to many others like you. My website is a book-related site. Using my URL takes you directly to my pages where there is very little evidence that they are part of a greater whole, but a visitor to The Literary Times home pages might also find my site. I consider this valuable cross-promotion rather than a disadvantage.

> Caveat: For this cross-promotion to work, choose a site that fits your branding image.

Before you approach a webmaster, consider the look you want. My webmaster, Tom Potwin, could have given me anything my little heart desired. I didn't want a site that looked like a news magazine—all straight and professional. I didn't want a dazzler— all lights and buzz and sound. I surely didn't want pop-ups (those annoying bulletins that appear on your screen unbidden and don't go away until you delete them).

I asked Tom to use a pastel background and muted letters. I also suggest fonts (type face styles) but such specific requests might not be possible if you don't have a background in graphics.

My site came with a long moniker (URL). I didn't do anything about it for nearly two years though I knew that I should. Not until I was asked to be an editor for Yarrow Brook Literary Review did I get a URL that was simple and easy to remember. The editor of this journal, Sarah Mankowski, took pity and gave it to me as a gift. She used http://buydomains.com. My URL went from this: http://www.TLT.com/authors/carolynhowardjohnson.htm to this: http://carolynhowardjohnson.com. You can see why the address is important. I am embarrassed when I think about how difficult it was for me to give a radio audience in New York my URL when I was being interviewed by early morning hosts at 5 am Pacific time with no caffeine fix.

> Hint: Authors' Guild recently brought action on behalf of a number of its members against a business that cyber squats (registers domain names of famous people to sell back to them at exorbitant prices). You'll want to register your name early so you can avoid this headache.

At first I submitted changes to my site piecemeal. After a while, I realized that it would solve lots of communication problems if I kept a record of each page in my computer and resubmitted the whole page with the corrections or additions made every time that needed to be done. I insert award logos, banners, artwork, etc., using Word (the only program I shall ever be proficient in), proofread and then pass it on to Tom as an attachment. He does his magic and voila!

I use another site for additional exposure and for the networking it affords. Authors Den requires a little more computer expertise but if I can do it, just about anyone can. Check it out at www.authorsden.com/carolynhowardjohnson. You'll see it has a place to post media releases, event announcements, books, articles, poetry and more. AOL has a similar service at no extra cost to its members. Other services may have similar perks at no cost.

Basic Guidelines for Your Own Site

I am including guidelines so you can take baby steps toward developing your first home page; it is essential that you follow protocol until you are adept enough to break rules without causing confusion for your Web visitors:
- Include a picture of you and your book cover. Both should be available for copy and paste by editors and other webmasters.

- For readability allow plenty of open space on your pages.
- Include a blurb or two about your work, even if you must rely on readers' quotes rather than those of celebrities or other authors (see chapter 12 and the index for other references to blurbs).
- When making decisions, consider your branding (see chapter two). Personalize your pages with color, logo, layout, and writing style.
- Choose a title for your site that will work well into the future. Don't use your first book's title unless that name will fit your site after you have published again. As an example, I titled mine THIS IS THE PLACE, because I didn't know any better. As it turns out it worked for my website because it is a metaphor that operates at several levels. But what if my book had been called *Shades of Irises,* which was its working title? That hardly would have worked as my writing took different turns. Your website will gain exposure on search engines, at least in part, by the title; you won't want to change it mid career because you'll lose some of the search engine spotlight you've worked so hard to achieve.
- Your domain name should read exactly as your byline does. To register it, try ZDNet's Domain Direct.
- On the left side of your home page, include a list of clear links to the other pages on your site. This can also be done with tabs at the top of the page, although tabs are more limiting. These links might include:
  - A site map, especially if you have written several books or want to include several different facets of your professional or writing career.
  - Peter Bowerman, an author who struck gold with three major book clubs, notes that most authors' websites don't have an FAQ (Frequently Asked Questions) section. I don't but I intend to work on it. (If you don't know what those questions are now, it won't be long before you will.)
  - A first person essay (see chapter three). Include permission to reprint without permission with guidelines for doing so.
  - A prologue, first chapter or excerpt from your book(s). This is your writing sample or teaser for readers.
  - As soon as you have a short slate of articles published about you and your book, interviews on TV and radio,

or other credits add those. They are, in effect, your references for editors, producers and readers.

- Add a links page. This page should not be a mish-mash of URLs for unrelated sites. Give it a theme or make it into a useful reference for the kind of readers you would like to attract. It might include links to all the sites you review for or recommendations for sites your readers might use to further research the subject matter of your book. For example, if your book is about weaving, a list of good warp and woof type sites will work as a reference page for visitors who happen onto your site. Links that are categorized like this could eventually become such a good resource that it draws researchers to it. Each of them could be a potential reader or customer for your book.

  > Hint: Find out who is linking to your site and who isn't by plugging in your URL at www.LinkPopularity.com. Here are ways you can use this information:
  > - A site you work with or think would be an ideal partner should be approached with that very suggestion.
  > - Those who are linked should be thanked.
  > - Double check to see if the information they have on you is accurate and current.
  > - If they are already linking, they might want to post articles you offer.
  > - Maybe you'll want to reciprocate, let them know you did and make a new publicity conscious friend

- Turn one section of your website into a press room. This is where your electronic media kit should live (see chapter three on building media kits). This page or section should include:
  - A link to your e-mail address.
  - Recent press releases and, preferably, an archive of old ones.
  - A news section to announce future plans.
  - A place where media can sign up to receive your media releases directly into their e-mail boxes.

- A page of awards. This can be the same page you use in your media kit dolled up a bit for readers (see chapter four and the index for awards).
- A guest book for building your mailing list (see chapters three and seven on building mailing lists).
- A window for guests to request your newsletter (see chapter four).
- A blog. (See a brief rill on blogging later in this chapter).
- Offer something useful and free. The net is still—despite efforts to the contrary—all about the word "free." These enticements may include:
  - Promotional e-books.
  - Contests.
  - Your research and links page may be your best draw.

Caveat: To get the biggest bang for your buck, anything that you offer free must be promoted for it to draw visitors to your site.

Possibilities for flavoring your own site with attractive and useful features are endless. You may be as creative as you were with your book or present a basic green-vegetable kind of site. Decorative pages can be as professional as one that has a big business look. The key is to regularize the look—the theme and the formatting—and to keep your site current.

- Update when you have new news.
- Purge old information and dead links.
- Change promotions frequently.

Your webmaster can only be smart as you make him. He arranges the stuff—he can't make up information out of his head. If you are your own webmaster, you must devote yourself to keeping up with the basics and new developments in HTML and design.

Your Blog

"Blog" is a webby term for journaling but it can also be a promotion tool. A blog is like writing in an unlocked diary. It consists of regular entries (they should be frequent to be effective) that the whole World Wide Web can read.

To be worthwhile, a blog must include practical information that others can use, be humorous or entertaining enough to keep readers returning for more, or be something you want to do for fun.

If you start a blog early on in the publishing game and keep it focused on the publishing experience, it might not only be entertaining but it will be a helpful memoir for writers about to encounter a similar climb on that same steep slope. If you sprinkle in lots of helpful links and anecdotes about other authors' experiences, your contacts and support group will grow.

If you choose to blog for promotional reasons, situate your blog in a dedicated section of your own website. It will be another tool for attracting regular visitors who may become your avid readers.

You may prefer to enter a blog on a site that specializes in them. Check out www.kinja.com and www.bloglines.com. Feedster.com is a blog search engine that might come in handy.

An Author's Website Resource

By now you may have guessed my mantra, learn, learn, learn, read, read, read.

- To construct a website, try http://www.register.com/wsn/index.cgi?1|3910614238.
- Francine Silverman who wrote CATSKILLS ALIVE recommends that you read THE NUTS AND BOLTS OF AN AUTHOR WEBSITE by Chris Gavaler at http://www.writingworld.com/promotion/gavaler.shtml.
- Look up DO YOU NEED AN AUTHOR WEBSITE by Moira Allen at http://www.writing-world.com/promotion/website.shtml.
- Find lots of ways to get your site noticed with 101 WAYS TO PROMOTE YOUR WEB SITE by Susan Sweeney, C.A. at www.maxpress.com.

Sites where you might get free or inexpensive pages are
- http://www.authorsfederation.com/webpages.html, webmaster Bill Keefer.
- http://www.tlt.com, webmaster, Tom Potwin.
- www.wordthunder.com, webmaster Sarah Mankowski.
- http://www.writerpages.com/promotionpackages.htm, webmaster Kim Cox.
- http://www.rebeccasreads.com/admin/book_promos.html, webmaster Rebecca Brown.

- http://www.homestead.com and design a site yourself with their tools.

Your E-mail SignatureYour E-mail Signature

...you ought not walk
Upon a labouring day without the sign
Of your profession? Speak, what trade art thou?
William Shakespeare, from JULIUS CEASAR

Maybe, but only maybe, until today your name at the bottom of your e-mail posts was enough. Now that you are or soon will be contacting editors, producers, fellow writers and readers, they will want to know more about you. Use the automatic signature that most e-mail services provide to give them the information they want or need. Once you have it set up, it promotes for you—no cost or time required.

To create an auto-signature, use the Help menu in your e-mail program. Do a search for "signature" or "signature file." Use six lines or less. Once your book is released you can include a thumbnail picture of your book cover or a banner.
A banner is really just a long logo and shouldn't be confused with popup banners on hard-sell websites. Try these ideas:

- Change your signature often or at least every time a new promotional idea comes to you.
- Provide a link to recent articles that have just been written about you or by you with a line that says something like, "See what the CHICAGO TRIBUNE said about (use the title of your book, as an example)." The site link comes next.

  > Caveat: If you use links other than those to your own site(s), you'll need to check them frequently to be sure they are still "live."

- Offer something free to encourage people to click on the website link in your signature.
- Are you an expert? Let 'em know! "Expert on publicity, media relations..."
- Use a brief invitation to upcoming public appearances such as "Visit my booth at the Virginia Book Fair," with a link for more information, of course.

- Design your signature so it blends with your branding. To quote my mother, "You wouldn't wear a polka dot blouse with a plaid skirt, now would you?"

> Caveat: When you send out media releases, queries, or submissions to unknown editors, remove art or photos from your signature. They may render the message unreadable for certain servers and editors may not want to risk a virus by opening your mail.

Chapter 7: Your Personal Mailing List

An emerging author awaits her first book with anticipation. Its look, its feel, its smell. She forgets the shabby book tucked in a forgotten corner of her desk; that book—an address book or diary—was likely her first.

CHJ

Your address book, whether an electronic list or a lovely indexed miniature you keep in your brief case, may be the most important one you own. In terms of promotion, it gets a five-star review.

When Collette Inez's FAMILY LIFE was published she had collected a list of 500 names. Twenty-five percent of those who were notified about its publication responded. This is typical compared to two to five percent from a "cold" list. In the March/April 2003 issue of POETS & WRITERS, Robert McDowell said that Inez thought of her list as a living organism.

How very unusual it is for an author to enter the publishing arena so well prepared. Rarely does an author know how important this list-building thing is. Rarely does she start collecting names, addresses, zips and e-mails early enough to boot up her publicity campaign early on when it can do the most good.

Because I had experience with mailing lists both as a publicist and as a retailer, I knew their value and I credit that list with turning my first novel into a Mille Club Book, an award given by my publisher for sales and marketing, in its first year. Don't delay! Begin to build yours now. I suspect that Inez and I were ready with lists not because we are smarter than the average author but because we were lucky enough to be exposed to the importance of list-building long before our books were ready for print.

A knock-'em-dead personal mailing list will be more effective than any list you buy and will make any promotion you choose—from your launch to your speaking engagements—more successful.

Begin by assembling old, hand-written lists and directories. Eventually you'll need a database like Excel or Outlook Contacts. You need a program that will accommodate a huge list because yours will grow as quickly as well-fertilized summer squash plants. You'll feed it with one name at a time. This is your small plot, your victory garden. Consider:

- Your starter kit will include names from old lists, new activities and a few from your friends and relatives. Search for:
    - Lists from high school and college alumna groups.
    - The parent list from your children's schools.
    - Country club lists.
    - Your Christmas list.
    - Your old Rolodex.
    - Lists from charities and service organizations you work with.
    - Local political contacts.
    - Coworkers at your day job.
    - Peers from past employment.
    - Cull names from the lists of close friends and relatives.

    Hint: If your name is in any directory, then that list is fair game for its members to be included in yours. Use it as a source for individual names or include all its entries in the list you are building.

- Code each entry so you know which list it came from. That way you can target your letters with mail merge or with a short handwritten note so that the recipient will know their connection to you.

    Caveat: Although, you are now building your personal lists, your media list is important, too; don't overlook or discard these contacts (see chapter three).

    Hint: Carefully code publicity contacts you're making now so that they can be filtered from your list for future media releases.

It is said that directing promotion at people who know us is 85 per cent more effective than any other kind of advertising. No one—certainly not a publicist, a bookseller or the people in your publisher's marketing department—will be able to build a personal list for you. Like writing the original manuscript, this is a job that only the author can do.

> Hint: Building a list is like knitting. Take a stitch at a time and one day, when you need a sweater, it will be ready to wear. After your book is published you'll have access to other ways to build your personal list; many of the people you meet will become personal friends (see chapters three and seven).

Chapter 8: Before You Sign the Contract

A verbal contract isnt worth the paper it is written on.

Samuel Goldwyn

Not only is Samuel Goldwyn correct in an oblique sort of way but it is also true that negotiation loses its potency after you've signed a contract in indelible ink on a good, solid document proofed by a lawyer. You might meet with success when you request a favor from your publisher but you can't count on it. The time to ask for what you want is before you sign. The trouble is, if it's your first contract, you hardly know what it is you want.

Some would argue that marketing support is a point of negotiation, at least as important as your advance; your royalties and your publisher's profit margin will increase in direct proportion to that support. If you want your book read, indeed, if you'd like your book to sell well, someone will have to market it. Now is the time to be sure that your publisher will carry some share of the marketing effort.

Hint #1: Do not assume that marketing support from your publisher is a given.

Hint #2: Authors who self-publish should not skip this section; it includes much that you will need to do for yourself. Those who subsidy-publish will find marketing processes in this section that are frequently ignored by publishers who should (or do) know better. Those who publish traditionally should ask for these accommodations before signing but, if negotiations go awry, writers need to know what processes they must execute themselves.

125

Caveat: If this is your first book and you feel comfortable with your publisher's offer, tactfully request these additions but don't jeopardize the offer with demands that appear to come from a finicky, volatile artist.

ARCs or Galleys

Unfortunately, many publicists hear the word "galley" and believe it is only an esoteric tool used for proofing a manuscript; it will, in fact, be as essential as a hammer is to a carpenter in marketing their clients books.

CHJ, from an editorial for RebeccasReads.com

If you shoot for the stars, if you want national distribution, your book in every bookstore on main street and more, the brightest review periodicals in the publishing business must receive review copies of your book. These may be in the form of ARCs or galleys.

An ARC (Advance Review—or Reader—Copy) may be a book identical in every way to the one that will eventually be sold in bookstores except that it is marked as an ARC and includes certain disclaimers (disclaimers are discussed in chapter 23).

A galley is similar to the printed proof your publisher sends you. It may be a bound or unbound pile of papers with your book set up in print in its nearly final form. It also carries information and disclaimers for the edification of reviewers.

Most of the important journals that might want to review your book require that your review copy arrive at their offices at least 12 weeks before the date your book is released. This is not a loose guideline. It is nearly impossible for a book that arrives later to be reviewed.

It is better if ARCs or galleys come from your publisher's office rather than yours. It will save you money and a book mailed by a publisher directly to a review editor will carry more cachet than one sent by the author.

Assuring that your ARCs are sent in a timely fashion may be the most important aspect of your negotiations. If your publisher is unfamiliar with the process, be ready to educate her; offer her a list of these journals complete with editors' names. If you are unsuccessful, it is then do-it-yourself time. Learn more in chapter 23.

Dustcovers

> The state of the publishing industry renders dust covers practically passé but for those authors lucky enough to have their book first printed in hardback, dustcovers make handy marketing tools.
>
> CHJ

The heavy paper covers that wrap themselves around hardback books are invaluable tools for your marketing campaign. Ask your publisher to do an overrun and supply you with several hundred. Of course, you can settle for fewer.

Specify that you'd like covers that don't have holes punched in them; if you can only get the perforated ones and not the others, settle for that. Publishers punch holes in their returned dust covers to protect themselves from fraudulent claims of unsold books. Here's how you can use these dustcovers when they arrive:

- Give away autographed copies at book signings, writers' conferences, your seminars and anywhere else you appear. Don't assume that because you are doing none of these things now that you won't be doing them later.
- Clip and cut covers creatively to send to fans, to slip into greeting card envelopes.
- Have covers laminated and easeled for signs. Offer these to bookstores and libraries.
- Your cover can be reproduced or collaged to your large posters and banners for a bas relief effect.
- Let your advertisers use one to reproduce a professional image for you; they will return it if you ask them to do so.

A Pre-Publish Offer

> It never hurts to ask.
>
> The author's mother and, probably, mothers everywhere

Because they are so profitable, many publishers do not have to be asked to send pre-publish announcements to your personal mailing list. These direct mail campaigns offer an Amazon.com-style discount on your book along with a warm greeting and a knock-out pitch. Determine if your publisher does this, negotiate hard if they don't but be prepared for a "no." Many publishers simply are not set up for direct mail. The good news is, this is something you can do for yourself, so save your toughest negotiating for more important requests. The advantage to having your publisher do it are:

- A letter from your publisher carries higher credibility than one from you.
- If the first mailing comes from your publisher, you can follow up in eight weeks with one of your own without overkill.
- If your publisher does it, you save and can use the money somewhere else.

Targeted mailings have more proven, effective return rates than any other kind of promotion. Four-color postcards work best but your publisher may prefer the professional quality of a business letter in a number 10 envelope. Either approach is better than not doing it at all. Oh! Negotiate for the quantity, too. Your publisher may assume you only have a hundred or so names. You are going to surprise her with your marketing expertise right now, before the contract is signed.

A Book Tour

> If authors, not publishers, planned book tours, book tours would die a natural death.
>
> CHJ

If your negotiations for other aspects of a promotion campaign go nowhere, maybe you could trade off their half-hearted effort at a book tour that some publishers offer for something more effective. I know. How can you give up book tour? You've always dreamed of a book tour! The hard fact is that book signings held anywhere but your own stomping grounds don't sell many books and they don't generate any big-time publicity because they aren't scintillating news (see chapter 30).

> Caveat: If your publisher backs up your tour with tons of paid advertising, a budget of $20,000 or more, and lots of support from their marketing department, you might find a tour fun and even profitable.

Advertising

> Like propaganda generally, advertising must thus pervade the atmosphere...
>
> Mark Crispin Miller, U.S. educator, media critic

Advertising is paid for exposure and, even in small, locally distributed newspapers and air spots, are expensive. Big ads splashed everywhere is the dream for most authors and most marketers. If an ad campaign is in the offing, your publisher may have a strategy in mind, but don't fault them if they don't. If I had a genie who would grant my wishes, I'd want full-page ads in the most prominent book review sections and magazines. If "Jeanie" would let me choose my top five they would be:

- PUBLISHERS WEEKLY, because booksellers pay attention to PW.
- THE NEW YORK TIMES BOOK REVIEW, because those in the publishing industry read it and New Yorkers read during their long, cold winters.
- THE LA TIMES BOOK REVIEW, because LA is my home turf and this kind of exposure would let me propel the ad into more features, more readings, more, more, more! Here. Where I can find the time and money to utilize that buzz to its fullest.
- TIME MAGAZINE, because they have avid readers and offer advertisers a way to buy space regionally.
- THE LIBRARY JOURNAL, because librarians trust it for acquisitions advice.

Depending on your location, the subject of your book and other factors, your wish list might be very different. If your book is about classic cars, you may dream of an ad in ROAD AND TRACK. Because this book's audience is authors, I'd be keen about an ad in POETS & WRITERS and THE NEW YORKER.

Now that we've done with our dreaming, this is the truth of the matter: Unless you or your publisher has a huge budget, can afford big ads, professionally designed, written by the most talented copywriters, strategically and frequently placed, put this dream aside for later. This is THE FRUGAL BOOK PROMOTER, remember? Even the big guys don't know if paid ads result in big sales. Their effectiveness is hard to trace. There are better ways for your publisher to spend her money unless she includes advertising as an *essential* part of a strategically planned campaign. You promotion funds are better used elsewhere, too.

Section II

What Do You Do After You've Signed Your Contract?

or

How to Make the Time Fly

The time between signing with a publisher and the time you hold your book in your hands will be like waiting for your 10th birthday; no matter how close the date, it will feel as if it will never come. It will go faster, though, if youre busy planning the party.
CHJ

Chapter 9: You're Getting Started

...increasingly, publishers are giving the majority of their authors less and less assistance. When times are tough, publishers prefer to invest their publicity dollars in books theyre fairly sure will sell—big-name authors, hot topics—rather than in promoting lesser-known or new authors, especially fiction writers.

Christopher Dreyer in an article for Salon

Dreyer's lament sounds like an echo reverberating from the title of this book. Publishers do little or no promotion for emerging authors. However, even if you should be one of the few selected by your publisher to reap the rewards of a well-funded publicity campaign, you'll do better if you are knowledgeable and use all the tricks of the trade to supplement their efforts. Many of the biggest publishers, as an example, still use traditional campaigns and tend to ignore the Web.

Robin Maxwell is an author whose publicity savvy made a difference in her own career. Several of her last books were published with a fine, but mid-size publisher. For her new book, THE WILD IRISH, she chose to go with a larger publishing house (William Morrow, an imprint of HarperCollins). At first she couldn't convince this giant's in-house publicists to underwrite the marketing plans she had used so effectively on her earlier books so she began to do what was needed on her own. Her successes were so apparent that soon she had the support she needed from the same source that had refused it.

An "awesome mailing list" was the propellant for Maxwell's success story and once it was on its way, she was invited to speak at a National Steinbeck Center event in Monterey, CA and, with the help of an agent, her book was submitted to Katherine Zeta-

Jones to play the character of Grace O'Malley who was a rebel, pirate and rival to Elizabeth I.

Amy Ferris is one of the finest emerging authors I have had the pleasure to know. Her first novel, a coming of age story titled A GREATER GOODE, (available at www.amazon.com) was published by Houghton Mifflin. The publisher gave her great hope during her negotiations with them but then did little to follow through with publicity and she has been disappointed with sales. Ferris has all it takes to plan and implement a great publicity campaign but she didn't know she'd need to do that for herself until long after her book was released. She says it was a "missed opportunity. It had such huge potential to encourage girl power, to inspire girls to speak up, to speak the truth and to be heard!"

You may be able to negotiate support for your book before you sign (see chapter eight) but most new authors are fearful of jeopardizing a contract or they don't know what to negotiate for. At any rate, if you didn't negotiate or don't know what your publisher plans to do, ask. Using this book as a guide, begin to do anything they won't or hire a publicist to fill in the gaps. You'll find easy starter projects for the newly-signed author in this section.

Chapter 10: To Hire or Not To Hire a Publicist

A publicist, like an artist, must not only have learned her craft but must also have the proper brushes, paints and thinners to do her work. For your PR person, the credentials you have built and the contacts you have made are the palette from which she works.

CHJ

That the author must still work her marketing campaign diligently—even if she has a publicist—is part of what makes the decision to hire one so difficult. If she still has to face her fears, toil like a worker bee on a hot day, even after spending thousands of dollars on a publicist, what is the point?

When PUBLISHER'S WEEKLY writer Judith Rosen interviewed Lissa Warren about her publicity efforts for THE SAVVY AUTHOR'S GUIDE TO BOOK PUBLICITY: A COMPREHENSIVE RESOURCE—FROM BUILDING THE BUZZ TO PITCHING THE PRESS, the seasoned publicist and author emphasized that, at a very minimum, the author needs to be "actively involved—even proactively involved."

Thus, even if you decide to hire a publicist, you must be prepared to do those tasks that only the author can do. Your book will also benefit if you determine to do the jobs that, no matter how savvy your publicist, you can do better.

Here is what a good publicist will do for you:
- You'll have a partner to share the work.
- You'll have her expertise and assurance.
- You'll have access to her contacts.
- You'll have a voice other than your own to laud your talents.

- You'll benefit from the prestige of having your releases and other marketing essentials go out under the letterhead of a professional.

Only you can decide whether or not to hire a publicist. It will depend on:

- If your publisher has assigned a publicist to you and her level of expertise.
- The budget your publisher assigns to promoting your book.
- Your available time.
- The calorie quotient of your wallet. How fat is it? How willing are you to spend your own money or use the advance you just received to publicize your book?
- How you feel about the skills and projects outlined in this book, especially those of traveling and speaking. If your fear limits your publicist too severely, she won't be able to do as much for you. Catch 22. If you are eager to hit the campaign trail, you will be less likely to need a publicist.
- If you can find a publicist who is familiar with books. Nay, not just books but the kind of book you have written.
- If you can, find a publicist who already has contacts. If she doesn't, when she sends out a release or a query it will be hardly more effective than if you sent it out yourself.

If you hire a publicist, be prepared to give her what she needs to work with on your behalf. Here is a quick run-down of where she (or your publisher's publicist) will need your expertise:

- She'll need your personal mailing list and the list of contacts you've made with editors and producers. (Both lists should continue to grow.) It's especially important that you watch for the names of both freelance and salaried writers whose work shows up in your local papers.
- She'll need your willingness. To speak. To workshop. To travel. To back up her efforts at organizing events.
- She'll want your input on current news when it relates to your book so that she can work on coverage apart from reviews.
- She'll want that media kit you've been working on; and if you've hired your own publicist, having it will save you money. If you didn't assemble a kit, your publicist will still need you to provide a bio and a sample interview page or FAQ suggestions and more. She can't manufacture information out of the air.

136

> Hint: Publicists familiar with the book business are not easy to find and most authors are reluctant to recommend them because of bad experiences or because they are acutely aware that the publicist who worked their book well, may not work for yours. Contact university public relations departments and PR organizations for recommendations. Once you've contacted her, ask for references.

> Caveat: Don't be surprised if hiring a good publicist feels like a recurrence of what you experienced in finding a good agent. You may be required to submit a marketing proposal and a copy of your book. Also beware the sticker shock. If a publicist is reasonably priced, the scope of her services may be limited.

Some publicists specialize and some are full-service. Some have tiered levels of service and charge only for the services you want or need and some expect that in order to reap the benefits of her profession you need to give her the freedom to run in whatever direction she feels is best for your book. Here are some services offered by publicists. Find out exactly what the publicist you are considering will do and what she won't.

- Most publicists are organized to disseminate media releases and query letters en masse.
- Their lists may focus on some of all of these: libraries, bookstores, editors, producers, charity and professional organizations and more.
- A publicist who specializes in representing authors may produce a catalog or newsletter for a targeted group of bookstores (usually independent) or editors.
- She may arrange book tours or have an assistant who does so.
- Some publicists concentrate only on TV or radio appearances.

> Hint: Jackie at Bryan Farrish Radio Promotion is an example of a publicist who handles only radio. Her contact information is: (800) 647-1315, Ext. 22, tk@radio-media.com. I found radio one of the easiest kinds of interviews to book myself and, if hiring, I would prefer to find someone with connections to prestigious TV shows. However, if time, travel

expenses and fear of a camera are considerations for you, you might begin your search with Jackie.

- Great publicists tailor your campaign to your needs; others may expect you to fall in line with the kinds of promotion they are set up to do.

Hint #1: Hiring a coach is like hiring a publicist's brains but none of her elbow grease. Judy Cullins does a fine job of promoting herself on the web and that is, indeed, a good recommendation for her skills. To receive her free "The Book Coach Says..." go to www.bookcoaching.com/opt-in.shtml.

Hint #2: An author might find that a mailing service that collates, stuffs, manages lists and has a close working relationship with an excellent printer is a reasonable alternative to either a publicist or coach.

Chapter 11: Marketing Aspects of Cover Design

But suddenly I saw the bright green cover
Of a thin pretty book right down below,
I snatched it up and turned the pages over
To find it full of...
Robert Graves

That Poet Graves is irresistibly drawn to a book by its cover is a reaction that all authors would like to produce in their prospective readers. Unfortunately achieving that response is no longer as easy as selecting a color; the design of book is now a task fraught with lots of commercial considerations.

For that reason, some publishing houses discourage input from their authors on cover design. Nevertheless, the design of the cover of your book will be important to its success and it's your job to take care of your baby tactfully but assertively. Make a list of what you consider important for your book. Request that your ideas be passed on to the artist or graphic designer for their consideration soon after you sign your contract and cross your fingers that the book goddess will smile upon you suggestions. This problem of control is one reason that some authors choose to self or subsidy publish. If your publisher accepts some of your ideas she deserves a note of appreciation.

Below you will find the four most important marketing devices for you to include on your book cover wish list, and one of them, you'll notice, is *not* full control over your cover design. I suggested letting your wishes be known, not insisting they be acted on. Authors must, after all, respect their publisher's experience and expertise.

- Ask for a title and a subtitle on your book, even if it's a novel. You and your publisher can do better than, *Shades of Grass: A Novel.* Your subtitle is a second chance at selling your book and "A novel" doesn't cut it. This subtitle is used frequently by the biggest and best publishers and, though I have my theories about why publishers are using it, suffice it to say that it has become a cliché that adds no real value to the cover of a book.

- Ask for a second subtitle and, if your chutzpah is at an all time high, ask for it to appear on the back cover of your book, left-hand side, right up at the top where a reader browsing through stacks will see it when she turns your book over to check out the blurbs. This is your second-best chance at selling your book to browsers.

- If you have been very successful at collecting blurbs, those laudatory quotes that are found on the back covers of books (see the next chapter), ask your publisher to include a page or two of them at the very front of your book. This suggestion won't work artistically if your book is published in hardcover but it will if it appears as a trade paperback. More and more excellent publishers and authors—both literary and nonfiction—are using pages like these to sell their books.

- If your book will be fat enough, ask for the title to run vertically on the spine. Have you noticed bookstore customers craning their necks to read the titles of books that are shelved? Imagine how yours will stand out if the title can be read easily because all the letters aren't lying on their sides.

Chapter 12: Blurbs and Other Praise

The business of blurbs has become nearly Biblical—
the giver of such guarantees gets as much as he
gives.

CHJ

A well-known author, Penny C. Sansevieri, says, "As powerful a tool as a celebrity endorsement can be, this is the most overlooked marketing aspect of an author's campaign. In fact, most authors I work with—even those who have spent years in the business— never give any thought to celebrity endorsements "

Endorsements are sometimes called "bullets" because they are frequently printed on the back cover of books with little dots. Sometimes they're called "blurbs." They are one of your book's most powerful selling tools. My husband is soliciting blurbs from VIPs in the Asian community for his book EVERYTHING ASIANS NEED TO KNOW ABOUT AMERICA FROM A TO Z; he has a few other choice words for blurbs because getting them from VIPs is so difficult.

Because most publishers use the term, I'll most often refer to these endorsements as blurbs. You'll notice how important blurbs are at your first book signing or if you hang out at a bookstore and observe the behavior of book buyers. A reader who is unfamiliar with a work will first turn to the back cover looking for these quotes that tell them something about the quality of writing or the author's expertise.

Taking a page from the Dear Abby-type columns, I am sharing one of my e-mails with you. I received it from a published author who is determined to do better with the publicity for her second book:

Author: Do you know how traditionally published books get the advanced blurbs from famous authors? Does the publisher go after them, or the author or both? Do the "famous" get paid to read the manuscript and write a blurb? How does it work? I have an idea for my book, but I don't know what the industry norm is.

My Answer: Generally, the author goes after them. A distant relative of mine works as an editor for a fine literary press and she calls in favors from her more renowned published authors. She is known as the pit bull in her office; few of her fellow editors take the time or have the tact and persistence to do this. Nevertheless, like just about everything else that publishers are supposed to do, it is best if the author chases blurbs down for herself.

No, the famous don't get paid; that would invalidate the authenticity of the process. The famous do it because they are charity minded toward emerging authors, because they owe the publisher a favor or because they feel the exposure will help their own cause in some way. Many of the most famous won't do it at all—it's too time-consuming to read a book with only a blurb in mind and they fear putting their names on something without thoroughly investigating it.

As difficult as it is to get endorsements, it is not impossible. Here are the secrets:

- Shoot for the stars, but shoot for the moon, too. In fact, go moon-shooting first. Ask for complimentary blurbs from locals, from teachers, from people and fellow authors you know. A few of these become ammunition that will help more famous celebrities see your project as something they want to support.
- Acquire blurbs by asking with a query-style letter. Let the recipient know why you value her endorsement and tell her something about you and your book. For her convenience, enclose a sample of what you'd like her to "say" in her endorsement and assure her that she is welcome to use her own words if she prefers. Find samples of blurbs at my website http://carolynhowardjohnson.com or in Sansevieri's book, GET PUBLISHED! Once someone has complied with your request, you may use the whole statement or extract a fragment from the quote.

If you omit words, use ellipses to indicate the omission. If you substitute say, a noun for a pronoun, or add a word to help understanding, put it in parentheses to indicate that those precise words were not part of the original quote. In your query include a self-addressed, stamped envelope (SASE) to make responding as easy as possible. If someone chooses one of your pre-written blurbs, remove it from your query letter in any future requests you make.

- Your contact may ask you for more information than you sent in your query letter. A synopsis. An outline. A copy of the manuscript. Accommodate such a request promptly before your celebrity forgets or changes her mind.
- Try not to be discouraged when your request is ignored or denied. Follow up with a phone call. That may be all it takes to clinch the deal.
- Each person who endorses your book has done you a favor. Credit her appropriately but also consider how the credit will be viewed by those who read it. *"Janet Elaine Smith, Author."* That's nice. But is she an award-winning author? Do her books fit in somehow with yours? Say both of you write stories based on Irish legends. Then you might want to list her as *"Janet Elaine Smith, award-winning author of DUNOTTAR."* If you are writing an e-book, it is proper to include a link to her site, http:// janet_elaine_smith0.tripod.com/.
- Once you snag a blurb from a literary or industry leader, try again those who refused or ignored your request. This time around, use the blurb you just acquired to convince your contact that you deserve her attention, that being included in your publicity efforts could help favorably expose her name, businesses or pet charity.
- Do not give up. When you read, watch TV, and open your mail, watch for new possibilities.
- Don't forget an immediate thank you note (see chapter 31). When your book is released, send a copy of it with another note of gratitude for the celebrity's contribution to its success.

> Hint: People who are writing an endorsement tend to be more reserved with their tributes than those who spontaneously compliment your work. One way to collect passionate blurbs is to watch your casual correspondence with an eye to praise. Save

compliments in a dedicated file and then drop the person a note asking if you might use what they said in future promotions. Opportunities like these increase once your book is in print because you will receive letters of congratulation, even fan mail. Yes, you will!

Here are some sources you might use for finding the names of celebrities for the endorsements you covet:

- The Screen Actor's Guild: Call (323) 549-6737 or go to http://www.sag.org.
- To find authors send an e-mail to the Authors Guild at staff@authorsregistry.org.
- Use a search engine to find writers. You may find their websites; there you can use their guestbooks to submit your request or you can write to their publishers or agents who should pass on your appeal.

Here are some ways to put blurbs to good use:

- Put them on a special page in your media kit.
- Use them in e-mail signature lines.
- Some make good teasers in taglines.
- Garnish query letters with a suitable blurb.
- Use a blurb on your promotional postcard, just above the book cover art.
- Use blurbs on business cards and other promotional materials.
- Use a blurb on the huge poster you take to signings and fairs.

Chapter 13: Your Professional Photo

You need not be picture-perfect but your glossy must be.

CHJ

Your picture is important to your all aspects of your PR campaign. It is not a place to scrimp. Treat yourself, your book and your media efforts to the best. The best is not the studio photographer in town who does prom portraits—no matter how expensive and artistic he is. The best for your book is a photographer skilled in taking photos for model's portfolios and Zed cards. She'll capture not only your features, but also your personality. She'll know where your eyes should be focused, how your head should be tilted. The glossy print you have made from her work will tell the whole world it was done by a professional though it is hard for the novice to tell exactly why this is.

I used John Gibson, www.gibsonphotopro.com, photographer to the stars. He captured something that no photographer ever had, even when I was young and had fewer flaws to conceal. John's in Hollywood, so you may need to find someone in your area. Be sure to tell your photographer not only what your branding goals are, but something about your book and where your photo will be used.

After John took shots of me, some with my Great Dane, Trixie, he provided thumbnails (easily 100 of them) and permission to have my choices reproduced by any editor who chooses to use it. He also supplied .jpeg files of these photos If you're not tekky, don't even ask what a "jpeg" is—just know that pictures coded this way are the ones that most editors want or need! I keep mine in "My Pictures" file to send to editors and others electronically.

A graphics company that John recommended printed my choice(s) from the many John took of me. Anderson Graphics (www.andersongraphics.com or (818) 909-9100) specializes in commercial photographs. They will answer questions and work with any author who is computer literate and can send images by e-mail. This is a quick rundown of recommendations:

- I had 4 ¼ x 6 inch images made. They are the least expensive ($52.50 for 400 black and whites) and they fit into a #10 envelope which is a postage saver.
- I also had a colored photo reproduced ($115 for 100) because I had a couple of slick magazines request them, but you may never have call for color.
- Your publicity photos should be reproduced with a white border around the head shot and your complete name in the margin at the bottom as part of the configuration.

> Hint: Minimum quantities from this kind of printer will be enough to supply you for a year or so. By the time you need more you may have changed your hair, lost weight or need a photo portraying a different side of your personality. A few hundred lasts a long time because you often send your photo electronically.

Chapter 14: Creative Promotion Items

Accustomed to the veneer of noise, to the shibboleths of promotion, public relations, and market research, society is suspicious of those who value silence.

John Lahr

If we don't feel our own product is worth crowing about, who will? Does silence allow others to ignore us? On the other hand, do we read so much hoopla about promotion that we believe everything is essential, including handing out scads of promotion items?

With the exception of small, quality thank you gifts, I believe authors will do just fine without purchasing promotional doodads, especially the kinds that get thrown away or find themselves all too soon on the bottom of people's clutter drawers.

If you do utilize promotional items in your campaign, I hope it is because you've found something memorable, something that works in terms of theme.

I thought of my first promotional item more as a thank you gift than as advertising. At the time, I knew I wanted something that suited the material in my book, but I hadn't determined that most of the "stuff" authors were spending their money on was not very effective. I chose a miniature thimble with Utah printed on it for my book's launch. My mother made little felt slip cases for them and I attached tiny gift tags with a quote from the book to each pouch. Mom refused to make more than the original 1000 pleading poor eyesight so my next promotion gifts were miniature hand-crocheted doilies made in China, presumably by women with no such excuses. My husband helped me tie tiny information tags to them with bows. These worked better than thimbles because they more easily lay flat in books, envelopes or thank you cards. But think of the expense! Think of the time!

I made these choices because each had something to do with the sewing imagery I used in both THIS IS THE PLACE and HARKENING. Linda Morelli (www.lindamorelli.us) makes artistic blank journals and notebooks by hand. She uses them for prizes and contests and tucks them into gift baskets.

The success of these items cannot be measured in dollars nor in book sales. If you must use them, your serenity quotient will go up if you look at them as means to promote good will and forget about measuring their effectiveness.

Choose promo items with care. Here are some guidelines:

- Shun the politically incorrect unless your book is a steaming gossip sheet. Avoid smoking accoutrements unless the title of your book is *Up in Smoke.*
- Hand or homemade items are appropriate only if those qualities are integral to the image you want to project. Unless you're an expert at design and printing don't make your own bookmarks.
- Editors and TV producers love food. However, your edible should tie into the theme of your book unless the food is a thank you after the fact.
- Buy in bulk to keep costs down but don't be overly optimistic. Your needs will change.
- Flat is best. Lightweight is a plus.
- Evaluate cost. You can easily give away thousands of promotional gifts and if you restrict distribution because of the expense, you defeat the purpose of doing it.

Bookmarks are the most commonly used promotional item. Authors use them as business cards, give them away at book signings, tuck them into books they send to reviewers and more. I have never used them; my budget got in the way so bookmarks didn't make the cut. Most authors, however, believe bookmarks are among the most effective promotional items because:

- They mail flat.
- They target the audience you want to reach.
- Many readers use them. Some readers collect them.

- They may be produced relatively inexpensively. Let your printer duplicate an image on a postcard and cut the card lengthwise.

Hint: Try www.modernpostcard.com, www.vistaprint.com., or www.megacolor.com. Expect to pay from $175 to $380 for 10,000 bookmarks.

Logo items from local printers or websites like www.CafePress.com are used frequently for mugs, shirts, hats, bags, even baby clothes. Often they tout that the difference between the wholesale and retail prices of the items will reap a profit for authors but this is misleading. Most authors find that their readers do not order this merchandise but some still find this kind of item useful.

Author of HIGHWAY HYPODERMICS: YOUR ROAD MAP TO TRAVEL NURSING, Epstein Larue (www.epsteinlarue.com), says, "I have two (logo) shops and have never sold anything from them. I like the tote with pictures of sell one right out of the bag!"

Logo items can help you promote:
- Authors and helpers might wear T-shirts to book fairs if that look fits their branding goals. Use both a head shot and your book cover for best results. Use a book-oriented quotation to broaden the appeal.
- Carry necessities to book signings with a logo tote.
- Kristie Leigh Maguire, author of EMAILS FROM THE EDGE (http://www.geocities.com/kristieleighmaguire/authorspage.html), uses logo coasters to thank event planners at bookstores. She gives mugs to editors, reviewers, and producers because these items might hang around desks located where other media people will see them.
- Use them for prizes and drawings.
- Use them for personal gifts. Your children will love having something with Mom's book on it.

Find unusual items in your local gift shops. When you see something that shouts "Zinnnnnggg! This fits my book better than latex gloves!" buy it as a courtesy to your retailer. Ask the merchant to put in its original box and then check for the manufacturer's name. Sometimes the tag or box will carry a website address or phone number. Call to get particulars:

- Before investing in a sample item, consider how easily or inexpensively the item will ship as well as its base cost.
- To buy direct from the manufacturer, expect a minimum order—anywhere from $50 to $300 worth of product at wholesale.
- Do not pretend to be a retail dealer. Tell the sales person that you are prepared to meet the minimum and to pay sales tax because these are to be used for promotion, not resale.
- Follow the rules of the retail profession. Don't ask for exceptions. Make it easy on the authors who come after you. It's Karma.

If you have no luck buying the item of your dreams from the manufacturer, approach the retailer. Speak only to the owner or manager and ask for a quantity discount. Expect greater cooperation and heavier discount for larger orders. Usually it will be in the 20 to 40 percent range and you may have to wait four to six weeks for your order.

> Hint: An item I found attractive that can only be purchased at retail is a battery operated, high-intensity book light that fits over your ear. Because it is book related it is perfect for people who have done something exceptional for your promotion campaign, and—unlike many other gifts, is suitable for men. Visit Kito Designs at www.kitodesign.com for a list of retail stores in your area that carry this item.

Learn wholesale buying, if you intend to buy gifts in large quantities. A couple of vendors to get you started are:

- Seek Publishing, Millersville, TN, distributes vintage cards, post cards and related items. They might be used to promote most any historical theme. $250 minimum opening order (smaller thereafter); (800) 826-4929; www.seekpublishing.com.
- Saro, Burbank, CA, is the importer I purchased many of my thank you and promotional gifts from: hand crocheted doilies that might be used as Christmas ornaments, coasters or book marks; batiste handkerchiefs embroidered with "Thank You;" Battenberg lace bookmarks, hand-appliquéd

tea towels, all for about $1.00 each. Some of these items, like the "message hankies" would be good gifts for most authors' needs because of their universal appeal and because they slip easily into an envelope. Reach Saro at www.saro.com. Or call (800) 662-7276. Opening order minimum is $100. Most items must be ordered by the dozen.

Hint: To learn more about the gift industry go to www.whereohwhere.com.

Chapter 15: Plan Your Free Ink Attack

Donald Trump s Business Rule No. 1: "If you dont tell people about your success, they probably wont know about it."

N.Y. TIMES Money & Business Section, March2004

This may be the hardest creative work you've done since you came up with the idea for your book so get yourself in the mood. Paul Bogaards, senior vice president and executive director of publicity at Knopf, one of our nation's finest publishers, says, "The biggest change in publicity now is that to reach the same number of readers you need more publicity." The best way to get that publicity is to know your book, know your audience and know what's happening in the world. To bring you and your book to the attention of readers you also need to know what intrigues editors enough to give you free ink and how to ask them for it.

Know Your Angles

Make It thy business to know thyself, which is the most difficult lesson in the world.

Miguel de Cervantes Saavedra, from DON QUIXOTE

To plan a publicity campaign you must examine yourself, your book and the world you live in differently than you ever have before. It is time to meditate, to get inventive, to understand how you can relate all these elements to your branding, your promotion campaign, and the lists you are building.

Think of the themes inherent in your book. *Where* is it set? In what *time?* What is its *premise?* What is its *genre?* As you're doing this be open to what others see in your work. I hadn't considered my first novel a Christian novel (still don't) but The Library Journal reviewed it in their Christian issue because of its tie to Mormon country. I didn't argue. Rather, I used this new slant to make new contacts. Here are some ways to do that:

- Revisit your book and your own little self—maybe you're so familiar with yourself you fail to see what might be interesting to others. Look for connections to what is important and current in the daily news.
- Carry a notebook dedicated to publicity; jot down everything that comes to you. You're searching for magic messages to give to editors and editors who will be charmed by them.
- Read everything with the goal of relating it to one aspect or another of your campaign.

Approaching Editors

> Attitude is everything. Do not harbor negativity about your writing or your ability to market it. Positives can become realities as easily as negatives.
> CHJ

By now you know something about writing query letters from this book including the sample queries in the index, and from WRITER'S MARKET published by Writer's Digest Books. Here are some detailed guidelines that will make your dealings with editors professional:

- Never tell an editor you want publicity—free or otherwise. Give them what they need to conduct their business which is to come up with interesting stories.
- Call the editor by name. Be sure it is correct. Mention something about an article she has written or at least the medium she writes for. If you can also relate your idea to what you know about her, so much the better.
- Keep your query to one page only, single space, with complete contact information in the letterhead, including an e-mail address.
- Use a strong lead in your query letter (see chapter three under "Advanced Techniques for Leads").
- Briefly tell the editor something about you, the author, what makes you an expert or why you will be interesting to her and her readers.

- Let the editor know what it is you want. Do you want to write an article related to the subject of your book for her? Are you hoping she will do a feature on you or an aspect of your book? Do you want her to publish the details of your launch in her calendar section where she lists entertaining local events?
- Thank her for her consideration and offer materials that may help her make her decision or help her with the job of writing the article. Something like, "If there is any way I can help you, please let me know. A complete media kit is available by post or electronically."
- Follow up with a phone call in a week or so. Ask if she received your query. Be prepared to discuss another angle that might interest her if she rejects your first.
- If you hear "no," be gracious, but don't give up. Try another angle a bit later. She may eventually come up with an idea of her own or later see you as someone who is quotable for another article she is doing.
- Use great headlines, e-mail and fax subject lines:
  - "Provocative Guest Tells Why Life Begins at 60" would work for an author of any kind of book who is 60 or over.
  - "Ten Ways to Get Even with A Guy Who Cheats" might click for chick lit.
  - "New Statistics Show More Books are Self Published than Not," might catch an editor's attention. I don't know if this is true, but it may soon be! Those of you who are self or subsidy published could use something similar.
  - If you are sending a query by e-mail, begin the subject line with the word "Query" and then add your great subject line.
  - Use caution. Misleading an editor as to content of an e-mail will not work to your advantage.

> Hint: Now that you've figured your angles, built your list and have a basic idea of what you need to capture an editor's interest, review the chapter in the first section of this book on formulating pitches. Learn still more from the 306 page book, HOW TO BE A KICK-BUTT PUBLICITY HOUND by Joan Stewart and Tom Antion. Order or see a sample chapter at www.publicityhound.com/publicity/publicityhound.htm.

Chapter 16: Your Professional Mailing Lists

Your media contacts are the jewels in your publicity crown.

CHJ, from "Inside Retailing," column for HOME DÉCOR BUYER

Remember that personal mailing list I encouraged you to build? Your professional mailing list will include those names plus your media contacts, bookstores and your readers. Yes, you will have readers, lots of them!

Your data base should be set up in a form readily used by mail services Before you begin to design yours, call such a service to ask for parameters. Do this even if you plan to do your own mailing. When your list reaches 5,000 or more, it will be more cost-effective to outsource this task and you won't want to reformulate the structure of your list.

> Hint: John Kremer (johnkremer@bookmarket.com) keeps a special list of his top contacts. He calls it the "Kremer 100." Yours will be named after you, of course. Kremer nurtures these contacts, "works them hard." This approach keeps you focused on your most desirable and receptive contacts. For most authors it will include their local media contacts. Using 100 instead of a handful of familiar editors, forces you to think beyond the easy and evident.
>
> Caveat #1: Don't let this Big 100 keep you from extending your list beyond the 100 when you have major news to disseminate.
>
> Caveat #2: Don't let this trick blind you to being flexible. You might end up with lists for your top 100 media and another for your top 100 bookstores.

157

Here are some list management tips:
- Keep all entries up to date by adding, purging and correcting.
- Keep your list current by occasionally sending out postcards (see chapter 17) as part of your marketing plan. Print your return address next to the stamp or bulk mail imprint and the post office will return those that are undeliverable. You adjust your list accordingly.
- Code each entry. Use a separate cell in your data base to accommodate codes. Each aspect of your publicity campaign will have its own separate code. These become useful as you begin to fine-tune your promotions. The codes will indicate the kind of pitch you'll use and help you filter contacts that it best targets. Little by little I increased my codes to some 25 but I started out with a few broad categories like Utah, Senior, Literary, Historical, Women. These are akin to keywords you might use for your book on websites.

> Hint: If you come up with several categories for a single name, code them all.

- Build lists as you go. If you let names stack up, you'll forget how you wanted to code them.

Now you're published you can add media contacts in new ways:
- Consider purchasing lists. Dan Poynter offers several kinds of lists related to book promotion. He assures his clients that they are up to date. Find this service at http://parapub.com/maillist.cfm
- Remember to add your reviewers and interviewers.
- When you read or watch TV, pay attention. Get names from bylines, the staff directories of periodicals, websites, TV and radio credits including hosts, columnists, and producers.
- Add writer friends you meet on the Web.
- When I travel I try to find at least one local program or newspaper that might be interested in what I do. I check out local periodicals. This information is usually available elsewhere but when I have a copy I can better determine suitability and sometimes think of a slant that I wouldn't have otherwise. A recent copy can also be used to update information that may already be in your files.

- Comb through BACON'S MEDIA SOURCE at the library. To save time, enter the contacts you find there directly into a laptop or purchase a disk of contacts at www.bacons.com. Be sure to look for book-related media as well as trade journals associated in even the most oblique way with the subject of your book.

> Hint: Freelancers write for more than one magazine, newspaper or site. If you can interest one in your book, it may mean multiple possibilities for exposure.

Here are a few organizations you might contact to get you started on targeted media contacts:

- A novel with an exotic setting or books tied to travel might benefit from information from the North American Travel Journalists Association (http://www.natja.org/).
- If you need a contact overseas try: http://www.internet-resources.com/writers/wrlinks-orgs.htm.
- If you've written a book that might interest the business community, try The Society of American Business Editors and Writers at http://www.sabew.org.
- If your book is science-related, go to http://www.nasw.org/
.
- You've written a how-to book for writers or a novel with a journalist as a protagonist? Go to http://www.internet-resources.com/writers/wrlinks-USAorgs.htm.
- For talk radio contacts check out www.radiolocator.com.

Treat Readers' Names Like Collectibles

> A great writer creates a world of his own and his readers are proud to live in it.
> Cyril Connolly, British critic

What if you decide not to lift a finger to promote? Could you, would you then neglect your reader? Or do you consider her as important to your writing health as writing itself? I'm always surprised when I hear of a superstar who does not respect her fans. I'm amazed when an emerging celebrity doesn't take time to coddle her public. A reader is an author's reason for being.

So when a fan asks for your signature, treat her like the treasure she is. Ask for her autograph in return. And her e-mail and postal addresses. You'll find occasions to do so everywhere:

- Visitors will sign the guestbook on your website.
- Readers will leave their cards or sign your guestbook at book fairs.
- The people who come to see you speak at seminars, on panels, in bookstores, and at your launch want to hear from you again.
- Those who subscribe to your newsletter are your friends.
- Authors for whom you've written book reviews are your readers, too.
- Those who write letters of appreciation deserve to be included in your future plans.

To build a list of readers we must ask for their information, verbally, with custom-designed forms or with a guest book. We can also glean names from checks, but only as a last resort. It is more considerate to have a customer's tacit approval before using their personal information. In addition we can ask readers:

- For their preferences. What genre they usually read. If they are authors. When you post the information to your data base, use special codes for these categories.
- For their ideas. You may be surprised at how some of them may inspire your events—even your writing.
- Try to note whether the person who filled out the form, purchased a book and, if so, which one.

Capture the information correctly. Review the information your reader gives you for clarity as she writes it down for you. She will view your attention to detail as genuine interest. Accuracy ensures that you don't waste your most valuable commodity—the name of your reader and the information that belongs to her alone. It also minimizes postage expenses.

Design a form that records readers' names effectively. Take these forms everywhere you appear—from book signings to your speaking engagements:

- It should ask the person to print or force them to do so by providing regulatory boxes for each letter.
- It should ask for each individual piece of information separately. Psychologists tell us that a checklist for a client's interests is more effective than expecting her to recall her preferences.
- Include an entry field for their suggestions for improving your event or presentation.

- Make another field available for the customer to recommend an acquaintance who may be interested in your book.
- Does your reader know of an organization that would welcome you as a speaker?
- Having your reader's e-mail address lets you shoot off a thank you for her support instantly. It is not SPAM if she willingly supplied the address.
- Your printer can stack these forms inexpensively into pads of about 100. Pads are more easily used at events and stay looking neat longer.
- Ask for your readers' information tactfully. I knew I was sharing my Los Angeles Times-UCLA Book Fair booth with a pro when I heard Millie Szerman (www.StairwellPress.com), author of A VIEW FROM THE TUB, ask our visitors, "Would you like us to let you know about our next seminar? Our city mayor is coming!" instead of the ever-dreadful "Do you want to be on our mailing list?" People don't want junk mail, they want benefits.
- Let your readers participate in some way. Millie, who is President of New Directions Public Relations and Marketing (www.NewDirectionsPR.com), uses drawings to overcome some customers' reluctance to sign forms.

You may hear about consumer lists you can purchase. Although I don't believe it would be effective in most situations, an author would buy a list of names from companies like American Express or CMS, Inc. (http://www.mailcms.com/). You might buy lists of people who frequent bookstores, lists of people who live in a specific zip code, lists of people with a specific vocation and lists that can be mixed and matched. The most narrowly targeted lists are the most expensive but well worth the additional fees if this is something you want to try.

> Caveat: The results you get from the most carefully selected commercial lists will not reap the results that your personal list will. Purchase a list to use in conjunction with your own list only if yours has not grown to your satisfaction or if you can see a marketing reason for doing so. If the results from renting names are not what you had hoped for, don't give up on the task of gleaning your own.

To promote list-building skills set a goal of ten new names for your file. Reward yourself and your assistants with a celebratory latté when you meet your objective. B.F. Skinner, a famous psychologist, knew that learning occurs more quickly with immediate feedback.

Add Bookstores to Your List

> I sometimes have the sense that I live my life as a writer with my nose pressed against the wide, shiny plate glass window of the "mainstream" culture. The world seems full of...bookstores which will never order (my book).
>
> Jan Clausen, from A MOVEMENT OF POETS

Bookstores, particularly independent bookstores, should be on your list of professionals. You might need two contacts on your list for each store, the event coordinator and the book buyer. Each will be sent different kinds of mailings. I overlooked most of what good relationships with bookstores could do for my books, and I'm sure I paid dearly for it. Next time around, ignorance shall not deter me. Here are some different ways to obtain a good bookstore list:

- Buy a bookstore database. They come to you on a disc, as an attachment in your e-mail box or as labels. Either of the first two are preferable because the information can be reused and because it can be sent to you electronically the same day. Try Jeffrey Bowen at (800)733-6511. A list of 1,000 costs about $150. Mention that Bowen was advertising this special the day I found them and ask if they would extend that price to you.
- Use the yellow pages in your phone book.
- Use the research desk at your library.
- Use the search engines on the Web. Links to bookstores that are members of the American Booksellers Association (independents) may be found at www.bookweb.org/bookstores/browse.html.

Chapter 17: Use Postcards

> Postcards are simply the most cost-effective way to stay in touch with people who are important to your business.
>
> Larry Siegel, Pres. Siegel Marketing Group

Postcards are ideal direct advertising but they also make great invitations, seasonal cards and more. I've seen cross-promotional postcards in which four authors pooled their resources in order to have huge quantities printed—which lowers costs and to utilize one another's mailing lists.

I designed my first postcard with my book cover on the front, a border around the edge like a picture frame and a quote from the book at the bottom in the lower margin. Here are some other hints:

- On the back, leave enough white space at the right for an address label. You may choose to make this space a little less than ½ the width of the card.
- On the back, the left hand side is used for promotional information.
- Your return address should be printed on the back because USPS will then return undeliverable cards. It goes *next* to where you would place the stamp or print a bulk mail insignia and you'll need to use a very small font size. Remember the far left will be printed with details about your book.
- Leave some space on the left to handwrite a message or for what I call a "target label." This left-hand space may be filled with a label with a special time-limited message on it—one that invites people to a special event, as an example. Using this method keeps you from having to print a different card for each different mailing.

Because postage will become an issue for you when your list grows to several thousand, choose a postcard that meets the USPS regulation for their first-class postcard rate. It must be 3.5 x 5 inches and 0.016 inch thick. The downside of using this small size is that you won't be able to put as much information on the back, but they will come back to you when an address has changed. Postcards work best if they are part of a regular campaign.

Advantages to using postcards:
- They're appealing and quick—no stuffing or folding.
- They are less expensive per unit to mail.
- They are returned to you at no charge if you send them post card rate; this helps you keep your mailing list current, a huge savings.
- They mimic your book cover so that it will be immediately recognizable when your prospective customer goes shopping.
- They're fast to read.
- They get noticed.
- No formal etiquette rules are applied to postcards; that allows for more creativity.
- Postcards have more staying power than many other forms of communication. People may even post them on their refrigerators.

Here are three sources:
1. Meg Rottman, (mrottman@stylepr.com) author and publicist, likes http://ModernPostCard.com. They print 500 cards for $125.
2. I used TuVets. They charge $199 for 2500 cards. Ask for Henry Ayala when you call (800) 894-8977.
3. Vistaprint is popular among authors because of their special introductory offers. Find them at www.vistaprint.com.

> Caveat: If you use Vista, design your cards as generically or multi-use friendly as you can because when you reorder, even a minor change in the design will kick your order into a much more expensive exclusive design mode.

Chapter 18: Get Book Reviews

...newspapers and magazines are trimming back their review coverage

Christopher Dreyer for SALON

Like Byron, many writers are fearful of reviews and reviewers. He once asked his publisher to "send me no more reviews of any kind," and was sure that Keats had been killed by one bad review (which, we know, in retrospect, was not true).

Some writers—particularly those who have made it to the bestseller lists—believe that reviews were responsible for their success; many other authors have been successful without them or in spite of them. The truth probably lies somewhere in between.

What can't be argued is that librarians peruse THE LIBRARY JOURNAL and others similar to it and bookstore buyers pay attention to the major review journals, book review sections and the like as well as any hype the major publishers send to them. Most authors would like to see their books in libraries and on bookstore shelves. I'm going to proceed as if reviews—particularly rave reviews—are something you, as a promotion minded author, would like to have. However, reviews are only one form of free ink; an author who has difficulty getting reviews can use other means of promotion.

If we judge book reviews by how well they produce sales, they aren't all they're cracked up to be. Efforts to pursue book clubs, catalog sales, and library sales are more likely to result in dollars and cents profitability than reviews will. In terms of branding, however, reviews are quite important.

Finding reviewers isn't easy and your publisher may not be much help. Most large publishers understand that the prestigious review journals ask that a galley or an unedited copy of a book be in their hands 12 weeks before its release date. My first publisher didn't do that; they supplied review copies upon written request from the individual reviewers. This is a cumbersome method. It is slow and it is more difficult to verify that the copy was received by a reviewer than if you send a copy yourself or if your publisher ships a copy to a reviewer at *your* request.

Thousands of galleys sent to the important review publications lie fallow in slush piles, so even if your publisher sends out review copies without being asked, the chances of having your book reviewed by journals, much less getting a glowing review, is remote.

It's best to assume you are on your own. This is how to proceed:

- Negotiate with your publisher for galleys to be sent to the major reviewers before their 12-week deadline. Some aren't set up for it. If, for any reason you are unable to get them to accommodate your needs, you can pursue other avenues like:
    1. Self-publish your own ARCs and distribute them yourself (see chapter 23). Most publishers own the rights to your book so you must ask for their permission to do this.
    2. Pursue interviews, feature articles, book clubs, catalog sales and reviews in less prestigious publications instead.
- Network: Join e-groups where writers chat. You may find a fellow writer who also reviews. Once found, don't be shy about asking. Personal contact with reviewers is one of the easiest ways to achieve your goals. Learn about author Elizabeth Lucas-Taylor's take on getting reviews at: http://www.authorsden.com/visit/viewarticle.asp?AuthorID=6472&id=9320. While you're there, leave her a note on her guestbook, tell her I sent you. Promotion is all about networking.
- Ask a writer friend from your critique group to write a review. Send her review to book, arts and entertainment editors with permission to print the piece. Be sure to include contact information. You will have better luck if you select media matched to the subject of your book or ones that might be interested in you because of say, your age, your day job or your past vocation.

- Do Google searches for lists of reviewers; double check to be sure each reviewer is still active and that she reviews in your genre. Your key words for a search might be: List + Reviewers.
- If you've had difficulty getting a site or newspaper to assign a reviewer to your book, try advertising. Most website rates are low (newspapers and magazines are much higher) and, though the editorial departments should not be influenced by the advertising departments, you may find interest in reviewing your book becomes immediately evident. Resubmit your request for a review after you've signed up for an ad.
- Subscribe to online newsletters. Pay attention to the details and you'll find sites to send a query to. Rarely will you find a direct request for books to review like this one from Dan Poynter's newsletter (http://parapub.com):

> "I want to review your books. Looking for fiction, poetry and art-related writing...Send book information with brief excerpt...to Christine Westwater, Book Review Editor, Writer's Monthly, ChistineWestwater@writersmonthly.com."

Once you have a review, utilize it:
- Ask the reviewer to post her review on review sites or to send it to magazines that publish reviews that are not written by their own staff writers. If she doesn't already write reviews, show her how she will benefit from the exposure. Http://www.blether.com is a site that encourages independent reviewers to post.
- Send copies of good reviews to bookstore buyers. Match the subject matter of your book to the product mix of the store; there is no point to sending a review on a psycho-thriller to a store that specializes in travel books. Go to www.MidwestBookReview.com and click on "Book Lover Resources" for a starter list.
- Ask your reviewer to post her review on Amazon.com and other online booksellers that have this feature.
- Send quotes or full reviews to librarians, particularly those in locales that have some relationship to you or the subject matter of your book.
- Use snippets from positive reviews as blurbs in any kind of promotion you do.

- Post blurbs from these on Amazon and other bookselling sites.
- Include the crème de la crème from your reviews on the "Praise" page of your media kit.
- Appropriate quotes from reviews might work in selected media releases and queries.

Many authors have trouble finding a reviewer because of prejudice. It is unfortunate but a reality that many reviewers (and others!) judge books by their covers and even more judge books by their publishers. If your book is self-published or subsidy-published, if it is traditionally published but printed with a print-on-demand press or if it was printed by a very small, unknown press, you may learn first hand about how debilitating it is to be judged unfairly. Rolf Gompertz, author of three iUniverse.com books, including A JEWISH NOVEL ABOUT JESUS (www.iUniverse.com), writes:

"You are so right regarding the POD bias and prejudice — do we ever get away from prejudice in one form or another? I'll keep your suggestions in mind from now on and avoid being specific in my taglines, interviews or articles, and concentrate on other means of publicity. I am reminded of the time in the late 50s when I started with NBC — how film stars were not allowed to go on TV shows, even as guests! The film studios were trying to "defeat" this upstart new medium, TV, and saw it as a threat to the motion picture industry! Well, surprise, surprise...! Same today with POD and independent authors vs. the traditional commercial publishing houses! They don't want to give up control — and the wholesalers, and distributors, and retail stores, and reviewers are all members of that same club. As you and I know, I am pioneering here and finding new ways of promoting, marketing and publicizing books, so that authors can take charge of their own destinies."

If your efforts to find reviewers don't succeed in big time publications, ask for reviews at fun, new places. Find them with search engines. Here are a few starters including some that come highly recommended from authors I network with on the Web:

- New Pages gives preference to independent presses, and is interested in all genres, current titles only. "Current titles" usually means books with this year's copyright. Send a review copy, cover letter and publicity information to New Pages, PO Box 726, Alpena, MI 49707. They also seek writers interested in reviewing others' books (see chapter four under "Write Reviews.")

- The Boox Review considers any book for review. Their submission guidelines are at: www.thebooxreview.com.
- Though I am not taking on any new reviews, try these sites where my reviews, columns and some rants appear: www.myshelf.com, www.rebeccasreads.com, www.wordmuseum.com, www.bookreviewcafe.com.
- Editor Tomas Scwell is amenable to posting book reviews on his site if they have four to five star ratings on Amazon. Contact him at: sharper@BooksUnderReview.com, and see the kinds of pages he does at: http://www.booksunderreview.com/Society/Religion_and_Spirituality/Christianity/Denominations/Latter-day_Saints/Arts/Literature/Howard-Johnson,_Carolyn/.
- www.ralphmag.org/sendbooks.html is edited by Lolita Clark.
- www.northeastbookreviews.com/guidelines/author.submission.guidelines.html reviews small press, special press and academic. Editor Tim McMahon rarely reviews fiction.
- www.bookslut.com editor Jessa Crispin prefers that you have your publisher send review copies if you want full consideration. If you choose to do it yourself, query first.
- www.silcom.com/~underthecovers.html#donate accepts queries and donated books to be used as prizes in contests.
- http://generationrice.com/forum/cgi-bin/topic.cgi?forum=12&topic=4 lets you post your request to the board, cross your fingers and hope.
- http://www.sfreader.com/get_reviewed.asp is a site that reviews science fiction, fantasy and horror.
- http://www.futurefiction.com/submission_guidelines.htm reviews science fiction, alternative fiction and fantasy only.
- http://www.vijayaschartz.com/reviewguide.htm is a site that operates like the big review journals; the editor suggests that you send a book for her consideration. I prefer the query method so that authors don't "waste" books on reviewers who have no interest or time but she reviews for several sites, so it may be worth taking a chance. Check to be sure she is a match for your genre; she has distinct preferences.
- Norm Goldman and several others review for www.bookpleasures.com.

- Laurel Johnson reviews for Quill Quarterly and Midwest Bookn Reviews (an online journal). Find her at www.authorsden.com/laureljohnson.
- www.romancejunkies.com/glossary.html is for romances only.
- Editor Louise Karcmarz specializes in "up and coming" authors at http://www.modernauthor.co.uk/.
- Query a new print periodical Bookmarks Magazine at service@bookmarksmagazine.com. (888) 356-8107.
- Suzie Housley, Acquisitions Editor for Jada Press, http://www.jadapress.com, offers four more of her favorites: http://dir.yahoo.com/Arts/Humanities/Literature/Reviews/, http://acqweb.library.vanderbilt.edu/acqweb/bookrev.html, http://www.complete-review.com/links/links.html, http://www.newpages.com/npguides/reviews.htm.

Chapter 19: Get Media Interviews

Attitude is everything. Do not voice negativity about your writing or your ability to market it. Positives can become realities as easily as negatives.Attitude is everything. Do not voice negativity about your writing or your ability to market it. Positives can become realities as easily as negatives

CHJ

I was dumbfounded when I was accepted for my first TV interview. I walked into the Glendale Community College's Public Information office, told them I was an adult student and that I was upgrading my computer skills to help with my writing and that my first book had just been published—all in one big, gulpy breath. The answer was simply, "Of course, we'd love to have you." This interview was aired on local cable TV and was taped using the school's state-of-the-art studio on campus by students who were learning skills needed for the television industry. I learned a lot about interviews from this experience but the most important lesson I learned was to muster the courage to ask.

You may prefer radio to TV as I do. I love it because show hosts don't care (or know!) that am wearing flip-flops, PJs, and curlers. Because most TV shows don't pay for hotel or traveling expenses, radio is far less costly. If time is a consideration, an author can often record two or three radio shows in one morning. And sleeping in your own bed and waking to a cup of steaming coffee is always a plus. The drawbacks are minor—getting up at 4 a.m. Pacific Time and trying to sound perky for an early morning show Atlantic Time.

Depending on your preference, use your search engine to find radio, Internet radio and TV hosts who are looking for guests. Compile your list and the next time a big news story that is related to your book in some way hits the news, send out query letters by e-mail or fax immediately.

Many authors arrange TV interviews in cities where they'll be vacationing. Others try for TV bookings in their home town and then fill in with national radio.

> Hint: When pitching for TV, be sure the producer "sees" your idea in Technicolor and that your idea is not only well-painted for the eye of a camera but well conceived to fit with current news.

If you have been writing articles (see chapter four under "Write and Recycle Articles") for the media, you may have an entrée with the editors you know or they may refer you to others.

Once you have been interviewed, ask the producer for a copy. In your media kit, mention that tapes are available. Good PR is anticipating what editors or producers need and helping them find it.

National Public Radio

> BBC Radio is a never-never land of broadcasting, a safe haven from commercial considerations, a honey pot for every scholar and every hare-brained nut to stick a finger into.
> Morley Safer, CBS News

Safer obviously understands a public figure's need for "a safe haven from commercial considerations." It is just what authors occasionally need to give them a foot up and our PBS is BBC's fraternal twin.

Lissa Warren, a publicist who handles authors Ann Bancroft and Liv Arnesen, says, "If you can get a solid national NPR booking, you can use that to get print coverage and sometimes, if it's controversial, TV coverage. It's not just a benefit of the NPR hit that you get. It's what grows from that hit."

Tips for Getting an NPR Gig:
Pitch a specific show. To do that you'll need to research what is available and also listen to the programs such as "Fresh Air,"

"Morning Edition," and "Parents' Journal" so that the idea you present to them is a fit. Listen to their webcasts to get backgrounds of the different hosts and information you can use effectively in your query.

With NPR you can interview locally and be heard nationally. Send your query to both the station in the locale where you live as well as to the producer of the national show.

Review chapter 20 on "Maximizing your Advantage" for tips on how to make one appearance grow into many.

> Hint #1: Pitch the shows with the highest ratings first because they may not accept a guest who has appeared on a competitor's show. If one of the biggies features you, however, many lower rated shows will be pleased to hang onto the coattails of success
>
> Hint #2: Find a sample of a query letter by Christine Louise Hohlbaum that actually got the author an interview on NPR. It's in the index.

TV

> Television is becoming a collage—there are so many channels that you move through them making a collage yourself. In that sense, everyone sees something a bit different.
> David Hockney, British artist

Because TV is such an important part of your quest for interviews, and because, as Hockney notes, it is so multi-faceted, I've given it a chapter all its own. See the next chapter for what you need to know about television's interview opportunities.

Chapter 20: Television

TV gives everyone an image...

Peggy Noonan, US presidential speech writer

Television is "a many splendored thing." Network TV. Local TV. Affiliates. Cable TV. Public Access TV. Each provides an author with its own set of opportunities and disadvantages. Authors on a budget will find doing radio cheaper and more accessible but the lure of TV will still beckon.

A big splash on network TV, say the Oprah show — even without the pie-in-the-sky hope that one would be selected for her now defunct book club—can make a book a bestseller. It is that dream some of us must chase.

The downsides of TV are:
- You almost certainly must travel to be "in studio" and that expense is rarely covered by either the TV producer or your publisher.
- You probably need to learn new skills.
- Unless you have written a controversial book or have a spit-fire TV publicist, it is hard to land a national TV spot.

It may be easier to start local and small for experience and move up to larger opportunities. I was once interviewed on "Coffee Break" by Kathy Anderson on WLTZ-NBC in a rural area outside of Columbus, GA. You may have a small station in your home town; it may be hiding in a strip mall, at your local community or private college, or in an office building with hardly a sign to identify it. It may be in a dark room with equipment that doesn't look much more sophisticated than those cams your 12 year old neighbor put on the list he sent to Santa. But it's there, waiting for you and your ideas.

Hint: If you appear on TV, contact the most suitable bookstore in that station's broadcast area. Tell the events coordinator that you will be mentioning her store if she has sufficient stock. If she doesn't, offer to bring some to her if she will set up a book signing. You'll be able to propel guests to the event with the TV show.

Caveat: When you interview, you may mention an event or sales information but inconspicuously, please. To maintain a good reputation in the industry, stay focused on your message and that of the interviewer.

Hint: An exception to my "Find other ways to promote yourself than paid advertising rule" is using the Radio-TV Interview Report (www.rtir.com) to let more than 4,000 producers know about your book and your expertise.

Network TV

> TV is show biz...even the news has to have a little showmanship.
> Paddy Chayefsky, screenwriter

Network TV is one area where a great publicist with a sizzling Rolodex can help you. When she lands you an appearance, though, you or your publisher must be prepared to pay your travel expenses. That is why many authors on a budget aim their network efforts at programs produced in their own towns or produced by their affiliates. That includes most news programs, a few early morning or late night programs and others scattered in between. I once was interviewed by Peter Kulevich on ABC TV in Palm Springs. I live within two hours of Palm Springs and my author friends and I in that area had a good old time sitting on bar stools at The Chart House watching Peter and me on the evening news. I got the gig because I was participating in an event to promote National Literacy Day. I had very nearly bombarded the TV studios with my releases and Peter had taken the trouble to check out my credentials on my website. This is an example of how publicity must be tackled from different sides—no one approach is enough, no one approach works alone.

To find locally produced programs, use your yellow pages or BACON'S DIRECTORY FOR TV. Bradley Communications lists shows, their producers, their direct phone lines and addresses, and even gives tips on how they like to be pitched. Go to: http://www.freepublicity.com/getontoptv/?10005.

Public Access TV: Your Own Program, Anyone?

> Bear in mind that you should conduct yourself in life as at a feast. Is some dish brought to you? Then put forth your hand and help yourself...
> Epictetus, Greek Stoic philosopher

One way to get what you want is to do it yourself. In some markets you can lease a half hour on public access TV for under the price of lunch for two. That's a year's programming for around $1200, cheaper than a single small ad in a metropolitan newspaper. Why do they do this? Because federal law requires them to; they don't like it much and they generally don't make it a priority that you will know about it. In fact if, you are interested in this kind of publicity for your book, you may have to dig—even prod—to get them to admit you as a bona fide show host in their market. This kind of TV is also called lease access and many who love books have managed to put together programs that showcase publishers, other authors and themselves.

Bea Sheftel (http://members.tripod.com/XXtildaBeawriter/write.html) produced a program called "Author Chat" for three years on her local provider. You might use a similar idea or one that ties into you book's subject matter—perhaps a show on handling finances if your book is Ten Ways to Financial Security. You could make it a series or a one-time special and promote it like crazy. The TV station will provide the camera, studio, editing facilities and—if yours is one of the forward-looking cable providers—may even offer free how-to classes in how to tackle such a project.

Connie Martinson is not an author but she does love books. She started her now syndicated book show using pure seat-of-the-pants motivation. Her story is an inspiration to those who want to try this method of promotion and if you should live in or be visiting the Los Angeles area, she is also open for queries at talksbooks@aol.com. Find her at www.conniemartinson.com. You might also enjoy receiving her bookish newsletter in your e-mail box.

Hint #1: Watch your public access TV; you are certain to find programs produced by others where the message about your book will fit; then contact the producer with a query as you would for any other radio or TV program.

Hint #2: Check out Celeste Resch's new WPAC Cable 10 TV Show. If you'll be in the Wausau, Wisconsin area, you might be a guest. Otherwise she may be willing to share her cable TV start-up experiences with you. Her e-mail is: resch@dwave.net.

TV Performance Tips

> The thing about performance...is that it is a celebration of the fact that we do contain within ourselves infinite possibilities.
> Daniel Day Lewis, British stage and screen actor

It is smart to take a moment to learn some basics before any first appearance, but know that TV is especially harsh on those who have not learned its secrets. Review these performance skills you have learned as a reminder before each foray in the eye of the public:

- Breathe deeply several times before the action countdown. It will lower your voice and you will feel more relaxed.
- Beginners should keep their eyes on the interviewer. You don't want the camera catching your glance following a distraction.
- If you have high color in your face or tend to blush when excited as I do, tell the makeup artist. She can tone down the amount of rouge she would normally use.
- Bring a copy of your book and place it your lap. When you want to make a point about it, pick it up and show it to the camera with confidence.
- Advanced TV performers learn to watch the camera lights and can then utilize this skill as a way to talk directly to the TV audience. Don't do this without training and practice.
- When a woman sits, she should cross her legs at the ankles. Men should keep both feet together on the floor.
- Choose clothing in medium or light hues. Avoid white, black and patterns. Select a fabric that will breathe under the hot lights.

- Don't wear epaulets or any design on your shoulders. If they don't stay in place, you'll look as if you're hunching.
- Avoid jewelry that jiggles or clanks.
- Linda Morelli, author of FIERY SURRENDER suggests women wear neutral colored fingernail polish. The camera person may take a close up of your hands holding your book. Long nails can draw attention from your cover.
- Linda also suggests controlling exaggerated facial gestures. She says she once "rolled my eyes heavenward. I've regretted doing that ever since."
- Be on guard before, during and after the interview. Don't say anything, on or off the record that you wouldn't say on the air. Recently even seasoned politicians have found that a live microphone clipped to their lapel can be a lethal weapon.
- The audience and the interviewer are friends. Relax.

Maximizing Your Advantage

> The advantage of doing ones praising for oneself is that one can lay it on so thick and exactly in the right places.
> Samuel Butler, British author

It is easier to grasp and control your image and message on radio and live performances than on TV. Radio requires only your wit and a lively voice. Photography, of course, adds another dimension but in addition to your image the producer may also be projecting other information on the screen. To manipulate your message on TV to your advantage, you need to not only respond well, but arrive early enough to know what the producer has planned.

- Make and review a list of the points you want to make about your book. Sometimes the conversation can be *very* tactfully directed to include them.
- Before the interview, ask your host if she would like you to submit possible interview questions. If she is open to that courtesy, you can literally design the content to meet your needs. You should be able to find a sample interview in your own media kit.
- If you arrive early you may be able to watch the interview conducted before yours, preferably on-screen rather than live. Critique that interview and adjust your performance accordingly.

- Messages like toll free numbers and website addresses sometimes appear on the screen during your interview. These are called chyrons. You want to know if these are planned for your appearance and precisely what information they will use. If no ordering information is used, your book cover or other identifiers may be. You need only ask and then adapt to the format. As an example, if they are running ordering information at the bottom of the screen, you can avoid presenting that part of your commercial message.

- Double check the need for that prop book you brought along. Look at the set. At one interview I did the producers had blown up my book cover and used it as part of the stage dressing. If I had been so nervous that I didn't notice, I might have used the book I brought as a prop. Because I noticed, I placed my book on the coffee table that was between my interviewer and me. It looked natural there but I didn't need to hold it up when I referred to it.

- Show that you understand the broadcast business by offering sound bites (clever, memorable ways of saying things) during the interview. Project what an interviewer might ask then come up with these small golden coins of wisdom; that's easy for you to do because you're a writer, right?

- Before you leave the studio propose a different segment, a new angle, or talk about your next book with your host or the show's producer.

- Leave behind a signed copy for anyone who was of special service to your during your interview.

- Morelli (http://members.aol.com/lbmwriter/romance/RomBooks.htm) brings a blank VHS tape and pre-addressed envelope with her. She says, "I asked if I could get a copy of the taping and received a quick 'yes' when they noticed the blank tape and envelope I pulled out of my carrying case." The tapes you collect can eventually be spliced to promote future appearances. You will hear these referred to as a "reel."

- Send a thank you gift to the host soon after your appearance.

- Follow up about four weeks with a proposal for another interview, one with a different slant than the one you just did. Or remind the producer that you would be pleased to serve as an expert on your topic should they ever need one.

- Send out releases about your appearance to your local press. If you can get a photograph of you with the host and a prestigious backdrop (one that says CBS TV, as an example) you could send copies to the press with your release.

  Hint: Radio hosts appreciate your tying something you say to a local angle even if you just mention their broadcast area when you thank your interviewer.

Chapter 21: The Rarely Traveled Publicity Road

The untried is sometimes true:
CHJ

There are lots of byways for publicizing your book rather than trying to cut into the fast lane on the freeways every other author and publisher in the world is traveling.

Internet Radio

Just as small ballerinas must begin practicing easy first and second positions before they can perform pirouettes, so must authors learn the unrelated skill of managing an interview in slow, easy steps.
CHJ

Internet radio is the new broadcasting kid on the block; they don't have access to the huge pools of guests that TV and AM/FM do. That means your chances of grabbing their attention are greater and with each appearance your entertainment skills grow.

Use search engines to find stations that will feature your reviews of others' work, that spotlight reviewers who might be interested in reading your work, that do author interviews or are otherwise searching for the kind of expertise you can provide. Here are two leads to get your started.

- Purchase THE ROUGH GUIDE TO INTERNET RADIO by L. A. Heberlain on Amazon.com or ask your library to order it for you.
- I enjoyed being interviewed by award-winning host Lee Mirabel (lee@wsradio.com) on WSRadio because she took

the time to thoroughly explore the subject I most like to talk about, tolerance.

- Leisure Talk Radio Network is a new Internet-only radio station based in Atlanta, GA that is adding programming daily. Check for likely interview possibilities at www.leisuretalk.net.

Classmate Contacts

Byrons great capacity for friendship (showed in his) generous tributes to old school-friends, and the outpouring of his heart in loyal affection

From a description of Byron in THE CAMBRIDGE HISTORY OF ENGLISH AND AMERICAN LITERATURE

Bruce Kimmel tried various ways to promote his novels, BENJAMIN KRITZER and KRITZERLAND, both "thinly veiled fictions" of his childhood in Los Angeles. It wasn't until he was "nosing around classmates.com one day" and found a message board for his high school class that sales took off. Along the same line consider class reunions, adding your classmates' addresses to your mailing list and sending your releases to your old high school newspaper.

Hint: Classes that came before or after yours may be as interested in your book as your own graduating class.

Donate Books for Contests

Give me your poppies,
let their radiance spill
rapture
for ever;

Hilda Doolittle, US poet

All kinds of benefits may trickle from a donated book to its author.

Once you start promoting your book you will find all kinds of places that not only want your book but will show their gratitude for it in dozens of small and greater ways. Sites like www.silcom.com/~underthecovers.html#donate run contests that feature books and authors. Sites like www.MyShelf.com run contests featuring recent releases as prizes. Do a search for others. In most cases, if you donate one or more books and perhaps a related gift, in return they will post a picture of your book cover and a short synopsis or pitch about your book.

Write Letters-to-the-Editor

The opinion of the strongest is always the best.
Jean de la Fontaine, from FABLES

Letters-to-the-Editor can be valuable exposure for authors. When you read the news, respond to issues that are related to your branding or your book. You might also respond to letters sent in by others that fit with your campaign. Here are some tips for turning your opinions into publicity:

- Sign your name, city and something like, "Author of *Politicians are Wimps.*"
- Having said that, don't assume that anything other than your name will be included in print. You get around such an omission by tactfully and judiciously dropping into the body of your letter the name of your book.
- After your letter has been published, point it out to a friend and ask her to send a letter in response to yours. If she is not a veteran letter writer, suggest that her correspondence will be more effective if she refers to you or your letter and supply her with the editor's e-mail address.
- Use a similar tactic when your name appears in any print media. Ask a friend or two to ask a question about the article or to find a reason to congratulate the publication on giving you coverage. Because newspapers don't do a great job of giving the arts exposure, that they ran a feature on you or your book is reason enough for applause from a friend.
- Some newspapers have special letters sections in different segments of their publications. Be sure you direct your comments to the proper editor.

> Caveat #1: Now that your name has become public, publish opinions only on issues that will enhance the image you are trying to create.

> Caveat #2: When you take a stand on an issue, be certain of it. You needn't rant but you are now an expert on subjects related to your book because you are published; so don't apologize or waffle. Bludgeon the words "I think…" out of your copy. Just state what you think, support it and let it stand.

Once you have become known to editors, it will be easier for you to contribute columns to the op-ed page or another section of a newspaper. Learn more about utilizing op-ed to create your image in the next section.

Op-Ed Essays

> Apelles, full of indignation, popped his head out and reminded him that a shoemaker should give no opinion beyond the shoes...
>
> Pliny the Elder from NATURAL HISTORY

You are probably familiar with the op-ed sections of the newspapers you read but you may not know they were called that. Not all papers identify these sections the same way. They are usually found near the letters-to-the editors section or on the page opposite from the political cartoon. Though they are opinion pieces, they tend to be longer than letters-to-the-editor and, most important, they usually carry a tagline (see chapter 21 under "Op-Ed Pieces") identifying the author as an expert. While the authors of letters-to-the-editor are not compensated, the authors of op-ed pieces often are.

Once you are a published author you will find it easier for your work to be accepted for this section. Find the name of the editor in charge of the paper's editorial page. Send her a query. Prepare with a convincing pitch about yourself and about what you want to write.

For op-ed, pitch an idea that is related to a current political situation or other prominent news item immediately after any event that corresponds with the theme of your book hits the news. To newspapers, the word "current" is crucial. Just as Pliny suggested in the first century AD, it is vital to confine your essays to those subjects in which you are qualified.

Chapter 22: Big Book Expos, Big Opportunity

> Specialized trade shows are big business. Books are big business. An authors own book is big business, too.
>
> CHJ

Many publishers and authors consider appearances at book expos essential to their marketing campaign. There are many trade shows and expos that specialize in books but BEA (Book Expo America) dominates the industry in the U.S. The booths are expensive but even if the cost of a booth and travel expenses are higher than your budget will allow, there are some secrets to putting one or more of these extravaganzas to your use.

BEA, the expo of expos, rotates each year between Chicago, New York and Los Angeles and is attended by publishers, librarians and bookstore buyers as well as the "accidental" attendees who shouldn't be there because the show is for the "trade only," but somehow get credentials to go. Learn more about it at www.bookexpoamerica.com, (203)840-5384.

Authors can use BEA or other expos to:
- Make contacts.
- Display and sell books.
- Sign their newly released book for the hoards of book people who attend.
- Get marketing and writing ideas.
- Have a heck of a lot of fun.
- Learn the publishing industry. Do this by attending the breakfasts, luncheons, or other scheduled speaker and seminar events and immersing yourself in the exhibits.

The book signing event is far and away the most important reason to get yourself to BEA in the year your book is published. Ask your publisher to send you but go into such a negotiation knowing that your chances are slim. If you decide to go—on your dollar or your publishers'—sign up early enough to assure your participation in this amazing signing event. You or your publisher must supply enough books to sign and give away to all comers in one-half or one hour time segments. Though I can't tell you how effective in terms of book sales this aspect of my campaign was because the results—like much publicity—are difficult to trace, it was one of my most exciting appearances. Signing at BEA makes an author feel like a star.

I have found that any exposure is—dollar for dollar—more effective if I can be in attendance to pitch my own book, but there are other ways to have your book seen. Writers' and publishers' organizations will take your book to expos for a fee. It is generally smaller than the cost of a booth purchased directly from the expo management. If traveling to an expo is too expensive for you or you don't want to give over the time to staffing your own booth during the expo, these organizations may be able to get you into the show, display your book and support materials and get you into the lineup of authors who are signing new books.

If you do go to an expo, keep expenses lean by conning a friend into putting you up for a long weekend, using frequent flier miles and bagging your lunch to avoid high convention center commissary prices.

Authors who do steady freelance work—columns or reviews— may qualify for a press pass which will save you the entrance fee and open other doors available only to the press. Your contact for this is Tina Jordan, Director of Public Relations (tjordan@reedexpo.com). You will need a letter of assignment on a publisher's letterhead.

Whether or not you are wearing a press badge you can take advantage of the press room, usually a comfortable lounge where members of the press snack, network, recoup and pick up media kits that they consider promising. Publishers and authors with booths are allowed to stock their media kits in an area of this room.

It is difficult to predict what a trade show or expo can do for you. You might get lucky. A producer or director might pick up your book to consider it for a film. If you are a great salesperson and if your title is nonfiction with an amazingly jazzy, current title, you might sell a ton of books or land a publisher. I met Dale Gurney (http://www.headhuntersrevealed.com/) at a BEA in Chicago. His book HEADHUNTERS REVEALED lends itself to outlandish promotion. He not only offered wild press kits but dressed in a headhunter costume with a hula skirt over his suit. He handed out fliers and left feeling like a winner.

An alternative to BEA is to arrange for space or rent your own booth at a smaller, regional show. Here are some leads:

- The Combined Book Exhibit at http://www.combinedbook.com.
- The Small Publishers Association of North America at www.spannet.org sometimes has booths at BEA and smaller shows that they will share with members.
- Publishers Marketing Association at www.pma-online.org.
- Look here for a comprehensive list of book related events: http://www.loc.gov/loc/cfbook/bkevents.html.

Chapter 23: ARCs: How to Get Reviewed By the Biggies

> Some books that have been ignored by the New York Times have become bestsellers; others that received rave reviews have never made it to that same publications bestseller list. It is all a game. We can choose not to play but if we dont, well never know if we could have won.
>
> CHJ

This chapter is essential reading only if your publisher won't send out galleys or ARCs to major review journals at least 12 weeks before your release date. Otherwise you will need it only if you plan to supplement their efforts.

Unless your publisher is among the most savvy, they may not be set up to distribute galleys or ARCs (an acronym for Advanced Reader or Review Copy) to review journals or, if they are, they may not be equipped to do it 12 weeks before your book is released. The big names in the industry require this lead time for your book to be considered for a review.

We discussed how to negotiate for this with your publisher in chapter eight, but if you weren't successful, it's do-it-yourself time.

> Caveat: Take on the task of distributing your own ARCs only if you are willing to risk the expense for limited results and if you are willing to take the pains to do it according to the firm and fast rules—from the media kit you send with it right down to the ARC or galley itself.

Making and sending your own ARCs and galleys may be done in one of several ways:

- Fudge a bit with your release date. Ask your publisher to list the official release date 14 weeks to six months from the day your first book rolls off the press. Many established publishers use this approach to setting release dates. This faux date is then used in media releases. Once your book is in print, take a few as review copies to send out immediately—yes, that's about 14 weeks before the "release date." Identify these authentic copies by stamping the title page with "Review Copy Only. Other Uses Constitute A Violation of Copyright Law." Keep the design of your stamp small and subtle. You're now ready to send the books out with your release or media kit according to each journal's guidelines.

- Have another printer or a subsidy press print a plain-cover copy for you. These are generic or plain copy ARCs. They may cost anywhere from $99 to about $300. Eighty to one hundred copies should be enough for a first-time author. I chose this method for my first novel. Your violation notice on these should read: "This is an Unedited Review Copy. Uses Other than Review Constitute a Violation of Copyright Law." The press that printed mine no longer works with individual authors but many fellow authors have used Fidlar Doubleday, Inc. (www.fidlardoubleday.com). They do short run printing of 25 to 1500 copies.

- You can make ARCs with your computer. To do this:
  1. Place all the chapters of your manuscript into one file.
  2. Insert page breaks between the chapters.
  3. Change your page setting to landscape (side by side pages on a single sheet).
  4. Click on Select All; it is on the drop-down list under Edit.
  5. Change the font to a slim font: Times New Roman, Arial or Arial Narrow.
  6. Change the font size to 10.
  7. Change the spacing to single.
  8. Todd Borg (todd@toddborg.com) used this method to "bind" TAHOE ICE GRAVE. These ARCs were acceptable enough (along with his writing!) to get reviews in KIRKUS and BOOKLIST.
  9. Clamp your pages to a book-size plywood board using C-clamps.

- Paint the spine side of the pages with a 50/50 mixture of Elmer's glue and water letting the mixture soak into the pages a bit.
- Let dry. Repeat three or four times.
- Then apply a coat with full strength Elmer's.
- After it dries, glue a strip printed with the book title and author onto the spine.

The final product more closely resembles a book than a manuscript and takes less paper. That saves postage when you send it out for review. Each copy should include the following information, preferably on a page of its own before the title page:

- Title.
- Author.
- Publication (release) date.
- ISBN.
- Number of pages.
- Retail price (the price a customer in a bookstore pays for your book).
- Trim size (the size of the book).
- Hardcover, mass market paperback, trade paperback or other.
- Number of illustrations and/or photographs.
- Publisher's name and contact information.
- Distributor's name and contact information.
- Agent's name and contact information.
- Publicist's name and contact information.
- Uncorrected proof notification.

Where to Send Your Galley or ARC

> The criticism of literary men who combine to praise each others works in press or otherwise...
>
> E. Cobham Brewer, from DICTIONARY OF PHRASE AND FABLE

You will note from the quotation from Brewer, a man of the 17th century, that then, as now, networking is the most likely way to get reviews. Most authors desperately want the distribution that they believe the best reviews will provide for them so they very deliberately go about getting reviews; most miss dreadfully because they don't know the rules of the game.

This is an arcane game. You send ARCs to two kinds of reviewers. The first group includes those who review for the journals you send review copies to. You or your publisher sends them with no personal contact other than your cover letter, fingers crossed. You do not send a query letter first and have no idea if they will review your book or not. You might get a review and never know it. If one of these journals decides to review your book they may assign it to a staff member or to a freelance reviewer who reviews for them on a regular basis. (I list some of these entities later in this chapter.)

The other category includes those reviewers you contact personally with a query letter. Some of these reviewers, even though they review for electronic journals, will review only from a galley or ARC. Occasionally one will accept your book as an attachment. They sometimes call these "e-books" or "e-galleys," which may confuse you, especially if you do not intend to publish your book as an e-book. When one is requested they only want you to send them your book electronically instead of by post.

You can find many reviewers in the second category on the Web by doing a search for both review sites and for lists of reviewers. Some review sites work similarly to the review journals, excepting that you submit only a query and then they post the request to a bulletin board asking for a volunteer to read your book. If no reviewer volunteers, you will not be reviewed. That is why you will have more luck if you contact reviewers with a personal query. Begin finding these individual reviewers at: http://www.lorraineheath.com/review_sites.htm.

Before you send information to any source, individual reviewer or review journal, be sure names are spelled correctly and e-mail or snail mail addresses are current. Here are some more suggestions:
- Do not use a media release when you contact individual reviewers whether by e-mail or by post. You may use sections from your release in the body of your query letter but use the query letter format with a personal and straight forward style (see the index for a sample of a query letter).
- Before contacting a review website or individual reviewer, read posted reviews to determine if the site is one where you'd want a review to appear. Don't query—much less go to the expense of sending an ARC—to a reviewer or site that specializes in mysteries if your book is a romance.

You are more likely to get a good review from a reviewer who has a taste for your genre or writing style.

- You may send ARCs to prominent booksellers—both those in your own city and national chains. Send them to the book buyer, not the store manager or gift buyer. Tuck it into your media kit. I'm thinking of publishing a couple of chapters of my next novel sort of a combination ARC and chapbook—to send out to a long list of booksellers as teasers well before the book is released along with a query for a signing or to conduct a writing workshop. You will find other ways ARCs might be used for promotion.

- In her fine article on ARCs Vicki Hinze notes that excerpts or full ARCs in numbers of 200 or more can be printed less expensively per unit than photocopying. You can read this article which gives more detailed instruction on formatting a mini-ARC and learn more about this award-winning author by going to: http://members.aol.com/spilledcandybks/ARC.html.

Here is a list of most of the important review journals that require a 12-week lead. Check addresses by Googling their titles and visiting their websites. Specifics can change overnight. An incorrect address or name marks your material as unprofessional. Be sure your book fits into the categories that each journal reviews. This list is a basic list composed with an eye to being FRUGAL. It can be expanded a thousand fold.

- **Booklist**, American Library Assoc., 50 E. Huron St., Chicago, IL 60611, www.ala.org/booklist.
- **Entertainment Weekly Magazine**, 1675 Broadway Fl 29, NY, NY 10019-5820.
- **Kirkus Reviews**, 770 Broadway, NY, NY 10003, kirkusrev@kirkusreviews.com.
- **Library Journal**, 249 W 17th St. NY, NY 10011, www.libraryjournal.com/about/submission.asp.
- **New York Times Book Review**, 229 W. 43rd St., NY, NY 10036, www.nytimes.com/books.
- **Los Angeles Times Book Review**, Times Mirror Square, LA, CA 90053, www.latimes.com.
- **Chicago Tribune Books**, 435 N. Michigan Ave, Chicago, IL 60611, http://chicagotribune.com/leisure/books/.
- **American Book Review**, Illinois State Univ., Campus Box 4241, Normal, IL 61790.

- **Small Press Review**, PO Box 100, Paradise, CA 95967, www.dustbooks.com. Poetry and fiction only.
- **Publishers Weekly,** 249 W 17th St. NY, NY 10011, www.publishersweekly.com/about/forecast-guidelines.asp.
- **Amazon.com,** Editorial, 520 Pike St., Suite 1800, Seattle, WA 98101.
- **Wired**, 16 W. 19th St., 11th Fl., NY, NY 10011.
- **Ruminator Review**, 1648 Grand Ave., St. Paul, MN 55105, www.ruminator.com.
- **Book Page**, 2143 Belcourt Ave., Nashville, TN 37212, http://bookpage.com. These needn't be brand new titles.
- The book or arts and entertainment section of your nearest metropolitan newspaper.

Here is a list of review journals that may be amenable to reviewing alternative forms of publishing:

- **Independent Publisher**, 121 E. Front St., #401, Traverse City, MI 49684, www.independentpublisher.com.
- **Midwest Book Review**, 278 Orchard Dr. Oregon, WI 53575, www.esecpc.com/~mbr/bookwatch.
- **Foreword Magazine,** 129 ½ E. Front St., Traverse City, MI 49684, www.forewordmagazine.com. Considers subsidy published books among others.
- Send ARCs to book clubs: Find a list at www.literarymarketplace.com/lmp/us/index_us.asp

Caveat #1: Many sources will not consider self or POD published books. If your publisher isn't traditional or if you are sending ARCs out from your home office, your job is to be so professional it will be difficult for anyone to ascertain that yours was not sent to them by the country's oldest publisher. Occasionally they will review a subsidy or self-published book and those authors so privileged feel it was well worth it to try.

Caveat #2: Some of these sources will also ask to see a final copy of your book as soon as it comes off the press as proof that the book was, in fact, released. Call or check each of their sites for specifics.

Making Your ARC or Galley Stand Out

Sending out an ARC or galley is a little like sending your first child off to kindergarten. She s going to

be making a first impression and you want to help
her along.

CHJ

To extend the simile about sending our child out into the cold
world, some parents are so anxiety ridden they overdo it. Clean
socks and panties and a nourishing lunch may serve her better
than fussing over buttons and bows. It's the same with a media kit
and an ARC. They only need to be practical and professional. You
can skip the frills.

Here are a few additional secrets, rarely used by amateurs, to polish
your presentation:
- Use a computer generated label instead of handwriting the
  envelope.
- Send your kit and book Priority Mail. It looks great, isn't
  much more expensive and USPS supplies the envelope at
  no extra cost.
- If a reviewer has asked for a copy of your book, write
  "Requested Material" on the envelope, but don't fake such
  a request. You won't fool anyone.
- When the envelope is opened, the reviewer should find a
  brief cover letter front and center.
- The media release should be introduced with the most
  powerful headline you can come up with in a large, bold
  type face such as "Sex is a Disappearing from America's
  Bedrooms."
- If you use a subhead (sometimes called a deck) under the
  headline in a slightly smaller size font, it marks you as
  someone familiar with publicity or journalism. This deck
  sets up a problem, such as "What will replace it?"
- Beneath the deck run a centered, solid line and use another
  deck with a solution that's a bit of a tease, such as "Many
  consider book on the new erotic politics a scorcher!" If
  your editor never reads any further, it's probably because
  she is already hooked.
- If it's appropriate, bullet the information in your release,
  much as this section is bulleted.
- At the end of your cover letter you need a motivator. You've
  seen "Call now!" at the end of TV sales pitches. Modify it
  to a subtle, businesslike statement. "I am looking forward
  to hearing from you. Thank you for your consideration."

197

Hint: Tailor these sales tools to fit your needs. Your book or kit demand heavy duty binding or cry out for dainty hand-stitching. Adapt each detail to the image your want to create.

Chapter 24: Library Sales

The serious writer would a million times rather sell a single copy to a library than to a reader for it is his wish to have his book read not once by one, but over and over again by many.

CHJ

Some authors disparage the sales of books to libraries. They believe that if libraries don't have their book in their stacks, readers will find it necessary to buy a copy. In fact, it is unclear which kind of sale is more advantageous to the author in terms of readership.

Generally, people with library cards purchase few books and those who buy lots of books frequent libraries for research rather than borrowing. The reverse argument is that though each copy sold to a library will be read many times, each one sold to an individual may get passed around from friend to friend. Thus, the objection voiced against selling to libraries is based on one or more specious arguments. It is best if an author concentrates on sales and forgets about how her book might travel once it is purchased for there is nothing she can do about it anyway.

For the purpose of marketing, getting your book into libraries helps generate the buzz an author seeks. Find out what your publisher does to alert library acquisitions departments and supplement those efforts. You can do a better job than your publisher at promoting your book at libraries located near your home.

Libraries are workhorses for readers; they might also labor mightily for you:
- Your local city, college and university libraries may support local authors.
- They may have a policy to buy books written by local authors.

- Contact them to see if you might be scheduled as a featured speaker.
- Get involved by offering to lead a workshop on the subject of your book or critique group on writing.
- They may disseminate or post your fliers.
- They may allow you to do a display in their window or on a bulletin board.
- If your book has a regional slant outside your hometown, get the names of libraries in that area from the Web and send them announcements.
- If your book fits into the classification of "mainstream," notify libraries state by state, starting with library systems that would be most likely to be interested in your book. Working one state at a time, rework your query letter to include benefits for each.

Chapter 25: Reading Discussion Groups

Avid readers are enchanted by meaning, which is available chiefly in books.

Mason Cooley, US aphorist

Many authors enlarge their circle of fans by visiting with readers' groups. You may belong to one. Members read an assigned book then come together to discuss it. Such groups exist everywhere, even in cyberspace. Often the author of a chosen book will visit with them, read for them and sign their books. This is where you come in. If you can locate one that reads the kind of literature you write, convincing them to choose your book is usually not difficult. They tend to be starved for contact with real live authors.

Find them at:
- Your work place.
- Synagogues, mosques and church groups.
- Women's groups and organizations.
- Bookstores.
- Libraries
- School and parent groups.
- Watch newspaper announcements and calendar sections for such groups.

If you should connect with groups like this, try to make your evening with them unique. You are not really in competition with other authors but if you provide an exceptional evening for them, word will get around about you and your book.

Chapter 26: Related Duties

> The profession of book writing makes horse racing
> seem like a solid and stable business.
> John Steinbeck

Once you are published, book writing is a business. Here are some duties related to being an author-business that need to be considered. Some are only obliquely related to promotion. Of course, it is difficult to promote if business isn't running smoothly, impossible to write or promote if the IRS thinks you have something to hide. These are only nudges with references for learning more.

You are a probably a small business now. If you'll be selling books on your own you need to look into local, state and national tax codes. Check out Lorna Tedder's advice on this at http://www.geocities.com/~lorna_tedder/virgins.html. Ask your library, the Small Business Administration (www.sba.gov) and your Chamber of Commerce to help you with questions. Keep impeccable records of sales and expenses and consider keeping a separate checking account and credit card for all book-related transactions.

Security-savvy authors get a post office box and a dedicated phone line. You will worry less about the attention that your promotion is sure to bring your way.

Keep a scrapbook. It's not nearly such a frivolous activity as it appears. The most practical reason for a scrapbook is that it will become one of your most invaluable references—after your own computer's hard drive. It will serve as a sort of résumé for future publishing and promotion efforts.

If you hired a super publicist, she would include a scrapbook as part of your fee and if you have a topflight publicist, her book will not be as detailed or personal as the one you will do for yourself. Have some fun with it; hook up with a Creative Memories specialist like my friend Debra Synott at <u>Debra4CM@sbcglobal.net</u> or check out the company's website.

Keep writing. I'd like to see you choose at least one form of promotion that keeps you writing. Promotion can get to be such a challenge and so much fun that your "serious" writing may suffer. Use all your organizational skills and motivation to carve time out of your schedule to finish your first book or pursue your next.

Section III

After Your Book Is Published and Ever After

*Great publicity is platinum. The golden rule is only,
er...gold. Treat your media contacts as they would
be treated but also ask what it is they want. You
can't provide for them unless you know.*
CHJ

Chapter 27: Is Your Book Ready For Its Birth Announcements?

There is no human failure greater than to launch a profoundly important endeavour and then leave it half done.

Barbara Ward, British author

The thrill of holding your book in your hands, putting your face close to it and smelling the ink—not in your dreams but in real life—is here. It's now time to send out birth announcements.

But wait! In order to start the countdown, you must have things in order.

Is your website up and looking good? You now have all the essential book facts so it's time to update everything. *Everything*. From your e-mail signature to your media kit.

Has your book been posted on Amazon.com? Is all the information correct? Is the picture of your book cover showing on your Amazon page or are they still using a generic logo? If not, Joan Moore Lewis, author of IN HIS CORNER: WILL THE REAL BILLY JOE PLEASE STAND (www.joanlewis.com), has used their self-correct feature: Go to the bottom of your own book's page on Amazon. Scroll down to the bottom of the page where you'll see a box headed with "Suggestion Box." There are checkboxes and a window for you to communicate with Amazon's customer service people.

Is your book listed with on-line bookstores other than Amazon? There are more—many more—than Borders and Barnes & Nobel so be sure your book appears at others including the ubiquitous

207

Wal-Mart. Check out http://archive.museophile.org/bookstores/ for a huge list of sites that will sell your book.

All of these sites are important for your readers, of course, but many editors and producers go there to find reviews, sales rankings, book cover art and more. Keep the horse before the cart. Don't spend time and money on publicity until your contacts can find what they need on the net.

If everything is A-OK, it's time to roll out all you've learned about media releases (see chapter three). Post your announcement about your book's release to these places along with all the other media leads you've been gathering:

- Subscribe to Book of the Day by sending an e-mail to BookoftheDay-subscribe@yahoogroups.com. When you post to lists like this it is important for you to write a snappy subject line using your name. That way you take advantage of the exposure you've been building on the Web before your book was published. Be careful to post to this group according to their guidelines
- Post-a-Page is good place to post book announcements but it will accept all kinds of legitimate writing-related media releases so keep it on your list for the future. Subscribe by sending an e-mail to: Post-A-Page-subscribe@yahoogroups.com. I get daily e-mail box notices; they keep me up to date on lots that is happening and it is easy to hit reply and then post my media releases when occasions arise.
- Sites for business news releases
  - http://www.comitatusgroup.com/pr/index.htm.
  - http://wwww.m2.com/Ms_PressWIRE/index.html.
  - http://www.Skali.com.
- These sites will accept media releases for book news. Post your release on them every time you have news:
  - http://www.eBookBroadcast.com.
  - http://www.localbusiness.com.
  - http://www.e-tradingpost.com/publicity.html.
  - http://www.bizwomen.com specializes in news about female-owned businesses. Yes, a female publisher or author should qualify.
  - http://quietpoly.com/bookstoresforpromos.html. Send your media release to Editor Sophia at QuietPoly@Yahoo.com.

The process of bringing a new book to light begins to feel more and more like giving birth. The big day arrives, prepared or not. When your book is delivered to your doorstep, life changes and you'll need to shift gears. No matter how prepared you think you are, there will be lots of surprises. Plunge into the next step with confidence that you are now better prepared than 99 percent of first-published authors and that what you know prepares you to adapt to exigencies. After all, giving birth almost always presents a surprise or two.

Your Book Launch

> A book launch is akin to planning a wedding. You may not need an elaborate canopy of wedding bells but all of the other elements that make a wedding a success must be considered for a launch.
> CHJ

Your first launch will not be easy. Launches may be elaborate events or little more than a festive book signing at your favorite bookstore. You will want to consider all the possibilities in light of your branding, your finances and your dreams. Your launch is the most visible part of your publicity campaign, its public foundation. Contrary to popular belief, a launch isn't about sales. It is about good will and planning a first step that you and others will remember.

It may give you confidence to know that by the day your book is released, you will have the roots for this day well established. Another confidence builder: Most of your associates have never been to a book launch. They may be as excited about the event you planned as you are. In fact Alexis Powers, author of PATHS TO FREEDOM was so aware of this that she asked each of her friends to send out invitations to a dozen or so of their reading friends. What a viral marketing concept that was! Her launch was the hit of Pasadena's social season. Here are some other ways to assure success:
- You started building your invitation list way back when you typed all your personal friends into a database. These names were your bedding plants. Now it's time for them to bloom.

> Hint #1: Here are some ideas not mentioned in previous chapters for finding people who will want to share this big day. Include people you've met on trips, in classes

(especially writing classes because they understand what you're going through and tend to be supportive), and your teachers all the way back to kindergarten.

Hint #2: Unlike a wedding, you won't want to prune your list, you want it to grow.

- Consider a celebrity list: You were so passionate about a subject that you wrote a book. Don't wince when I tell you to invite your local and state politicians, authors, actors—especially those who might sympathize with your cause. If just one of these people attends it will add prestige to your launch. After you've sent out the invitation and before the event, call them to see if you can count on their support and if they agree, ask if you can use their name in media releases.
- Arrange for a location of interest.
- Arrange to tie your launch with a charity—preferably something that is associated in some way with your book. My first book was launched at the Autry Museum of Western Heritage because it includes pioneer history. That interested the museum as did the fact that my book sales benefited their foundation.
- Offer something free. I gave away thimbles because of the sewing imagery in the book. If I had thought about it, I think a chapbook of excerpts from my book or a miniature book of recipes inspired by scenes from my book would have been a better choice because such a giveaway might not only be kept but passed along to others. Such considerations in selecting your favor are vital. Let people know about added values like this one, what you are serving and your program when you invite them.
- Use prior events to promote. If you teach classes, do any speaking, do a book signing or even pay bills before the event, use them to promote the launch. Tuck invitations the size of business cards or postcards into any mail you send out.
- Coordinate your contacts with the media. Send out your initial media releases (preferably a whole media kit) one month before the launch. One week after that, phone to see if your contacts received the material. Use the occasion to discuss angles that might be useful to them. Ask if there is anything else you can do to make their job easier. The

next week send faxes highlighting a different angle—perhaps the charity or celebrity aspect that you've arranged—and then one or two days before send out e-mail reminders. The final e-mail should be personal and include an invitation for these editors to attend.

- Your invitation list should be sent by post two weeks in advance with an e-mail reminder just a few days before.
- Use the occasion of your launch to update your list. Offer a drawing for something appealing, use a guestbook or both. A friend will feel honored if you ask her to attend your guestbook; someone to oversee it assures accuracy.
- Use the information you have gleaned with your guestbook to express your appreciation for support. Mention the title of your book in your thank you note and mention something about how successful the launch was. Send a gift to those who helped with food, book sales, your guestbook, and those who managed the venue.
- Serve really tasty food. You may have a friend who loves to cook who will help. Consider finger food and check with your venue administration about local laws governing the serving of food.
- Borrow a book on planning a wedding from the library and consider every element you find there, from limousine service and parking attendants to mikes and lighting. You may discard most, but you won't miss an essential if you attack this party like a planning professional.

> Hint: Keep up your lists, backup your records, make notes. That will make your next launch sweet and easy.

Chapter 28: Book Signings or Readings: That is the Question

To read, or not to read: That is the question.
Whether tis nobler in the mind to suffer
The slings and arrows of outrageous critics,
Or to take arms against a sea of potential readers/
book-buyers. And thus opposing, charm them into
buying my book.

JayCe Crawford, author, paraphrases you-know-who

Cold book signings can be really chilly. Our job as promoting authors is to warm them up but if you are not already famous or a dramatist at heart, you may choose to avoid locations that aren't on your own stomping ground.

I witnessed a book signing for Anne Rice at Vroman's Books in Pasadena, CA. People were lined up around the block—and doubled back. Her fans had been there for hours with Rice's big, fat books in hand—newly purchased—waiting for her to arrive. I was on the way to a movie. When I came out, the line was just as long—but the faces were all new. Heaven (and Vroman's accountants) might be the only entities with a firm take on how many books she signed in 1 ½ hours or how many more she would sign before her writing hand became too sore to function.

I mention this because signings have their place. That place is just about anywhere if the author is already famous. If she is not, that place is in the middle of her own little pond. An emerging author may have more than one pond—a small lake where she works, a small puddle of a community where she sleeps, another where she was raised—but, unless the author, a publicist, or a publisher has stirred up huge waves in that larger ocean —the national book-buying community—she will find that signing outside of any area where she is known may be discouraging.

Someday, after decades of growth, you may have a book signing like Ann Rice's. Until then, my own book signing story may be closer to what you might expect. My launch and the signings I did in locales where I had contacts were successful (by much more humble standards than Rice's!) but still tons of work and not much fun.

Before my novel was published, I spent almost three decades as a founder and owner of gift stores. I also had experience as a publicist. After that many years in the business of selling and PR, I know how to do both. Some people are good at these related fields, some aren't. Some like promotion and sales, others don't. Even with a strong background in both, I gleaned little joy from book signings excepting for meeting those who knew my work and came to wish me well.

That does not mean I have discarded book signings from my repertoire of promotions. I have, instead, set up rules that fit both my emotional needs and my goals for promotion. Aside from urging you to keep your signings within familiar territory, here are some of the other guidelines I have made for myself for you to consider:

- I'll sign, but to do so I must be a speaker, reader or participant in some kind of event. It is the only way to—using JayCe's word—"charm"
  readers into buying a book. The signing, then, becomes more of a party where contact and relationships are as important as selling books. To walk into a bookstore (or book fair, for that matter) without what is known in the entertainment trade as a warm up, does not work well.
- I will not think of book sales as the prime purpose for doing book signings—they are occasions for exposure in person and in the press, for branding and for fun.
- I will focus on one large launch per book, perhaps for charity, invite tons of people and have a *party.*
- I will only sign in a locale where I know people or have contacts that allow me to either get air or ink space from the event or that enables me to send out invitations in sufficient numbers to ensure attendance.
- I will only sign for stores that will do their full share of advance publicity. This includes:

214

- Exposure in their newsletter, in print or on the Web.
- Posting signs or distributing fliers or bookmarks in the store before the book signing.

Because signings are often the first promotion that new authors consider, I do not recommend traditional book signings in the course I teach for UCLA's Writers' Program excepting, perhaps, to say, "Maybe you shouldn't!" Not until you have a Rice kind of fan club, anyway." I want inexperienced authors to put on the brakes and use their energy where it will do the most good.

> Caveat: You may choose to do a full-blown book tour because it would fulfill a life's dream or because you believe your situation gives you a better chance at success than the average. If so, go at it full force and swinging. Take a card from the deck of T.C. Boyle, literary author cum promoter extraordinaire: In POETS & WRITERS, Joanna Smith Rakoff says he is "not content with nice reviews and decent book sales…he wants to be a phenomenon."

> That's how you should approach book signings if you should choose to take on that assignment.

Here are some ideas, in the form of a tip sheet (remember those?) that you can use:

A Dozen Ideas to Make Your Book Signing, Like, Worth Being There

1. Coordinate your plans with whoever is in charge of your bookstore's events. Let her know what you will need— both the set-up and the promotion.
2. Ask the store manager to occasionally use the store's PA system to introduce you to customers, especially if you are not reading.
3. Arrive an hour early to set up properly. Many stores will not have prepared for your visit, even after you discussed your needs with them.
4. Ask the sales associate at the cash register if you can stack some of your books on the counter. This area is called "point of purchase" by the retail trade—for obvious reasons.

5. Although some bookstores stock their own "autographed copy" stickers, have some made just in case. Use them on the signed copies you leave for the bookstore to sell after the event. Don't worry, you will use them all at your launch and other places you appear. I used one of the address label services I found in my Sunday newspaper throwaway.

6. Offer to send autographed bookplates to the bookstore manager when she reorders. Bookplates, an old-fashioned idea of personalizing the books in one's library with contact information so that they can be returned, can be purchased at bookstores in the new-fangled sticker variety. You can also use mailing labels. Authors simply sign them and the bookstore manager can apply them to the title page or inside cover of that author's book.

7. Design knock 'em dead signs. Verbiage should have the same level of pizzazz as loglines used for screenplays. Color is important. So is quality.

8. Put your signs everywhere. Post one on the top of a stack of your books at the point-of-purchase, a tent card on the shelf where your books are normally displayed, one on your signing table, one in the window, and more. Send one to the store to use at least one week before the event. Design these signs so they can be recycled for other events.

9. Take along plastic or wire display stands—they're like plate stands. Use them to display your book upright where there is little space available. To purchase them go to www.displaystand4you.com, http://www.footprintpress.com/stand.htm or your favorite collectible or hardware store.

10. Ask the bookstore manager, sales associate or both to train their salespeople to refer customers who go through checkout to you. They could say something like, "By the way, have you stopped to say hello to our award-winning author who's signing books today?" as she points to the pile of books on the counter or to wherever you are set up.

11. Talk to the sales associates. They are the ones who spread the word about books. Offer a signed book to a salesperson who is especially interested and ask her if she would recommend it when she is done.

12. Bring something to give away to those who buy your book, certainly, but also to those who pause to talk. All, excepting the candy, should include information for ordering your book on them. Possibilities are:

- A bookmark.
- Your promotion (business) card.
- A token souvenir (see chapter 14).
- A recipe. Even if your book isn't a cookbook, a recipe from a kitchen or cooking scene will be well received; it might include an excerpt or quote from that chapter.
- Give away a list: An example is, "The Year's 10 Best Reads." Include your book and contact information.
- If your publisher provides you with extra book covers, sign and give one to each person who purchases your book.
- Offer wrapped candy at your signing table.

Final Book Signing Touches

- Use a guestbook. Encourage people to list their e-mail addresses for future promotional purposes. A contest or drawing may persuade them to sign.
- Bring a friend to help. Her duties are to ask people to sign your guestbook, take pictures and chat with you when it is slow.
- Slip a snapshot into your thank you notes after the signing, use them for future promotions and for your own scrapbook.
- Review your pitch (see the latter few sections of chapter two) until it sounds natural when you use it on people who will be walking by.
- Bring your own fine-tipped markers for signing. Know what you'll write before your signature but personalize this message when you can. Always ask how to spell the purchaser's name if she would like the book dedicated.

> Hint: I bought a lightweight canvas bag with rollers to use as permanent event storage. It includes the items in both of the lists above as well as a small purse full of office essentials (see chapter five for a list of office supplies I put in the pouch).

Fallacies Regarding Book Signings

> Normally, people believe that, if they hear just words, that these words must lead to some thought...
> Johann Wolfgang Von Goethe, poet

Don't believe everything you hear. Be especially cautious about information on the Web. Listen, learn, but know that many authors and PR "experts" repeat gossip rather than what they know from a reliable source or from first-hand experience. Here are some fallacious "truths" about book signings that have run rampant among authors:

Fallacy #1: You can't have an effective promotional campaign without a book tour. Most authors today choose to do scattered signings, not tours, because most pay travel expenses themselves. It is less costly to sign in cities you plan to visit anyway. You don't have to do any signings at all if you prefer to vigorously attack another approach for your campaign.

Fallacy #2: If you sign books before you leave the bookstore, management can't return them. I have a big box full of books— some signed, some not—that were returned to my publicist (eventually) after a whirlwind of book signing gigs. They are physical proof that bookstores both can and will return signed books. And, yes, my publicist did have an agreement with the stores that signed books could not be returned. If you are unlucky enough (or unprepared enough) to have a dismal signing, be aware that the store manager will not be thrilled about keeping a half dozen books, signed or unsigned, in her inventory. Even if your book sales went well, follow-up sales may not match that success. A bookstore is in the business of selling books, not stocking them.

Fallacy #3: If you take extra books and need to use them, the bookstore will pay you upon delivery or within 30 days. I still have a list of unpaid invoices from the signings I did in 2001 for THIS IS THE PLACE. Rarely do bookstores pay in less than 60 or 90 days. Rarely will they pay without reminders. Never will they pay unless you provide an invoice. I always ask if a bookstore can pay before I leave the premises and had only one, R&K Bookstore in St. George, UT, who did so. And they offered before I asked.

Fallacy #4: You can ensure success of a signing by running an ad in a local paper or by buying a list of names in that locale. One hard-earned lesson I learned was how important your mailing list is—not just a list but a *targeted* mailing list. For my first book signing I used a list left over from my retail stores, assuming that people who knew me would be interested. Not true. Many who know you may not be readers or may not read the genre in which you write.

> Caveat: This does not mean you should not promote your event. Send announcements to calendar listings in local papers, pitch feature editors, use all your FRUGAL BOOK PROMOTOR skills and, of course, cull any names from your own mailing list that happen to live within, say, a 20 mile radius of where you'll be appearing.

Fallacy#5: Bookstores are the only venues for book signings. There are all kinds of places for you to sign books, places that you have personally supported in the past and that will, now, return the favor. Some nontraditional venues make signing an adventure and possibly more profitable. You will think of your own, but here are some suggestions:

- One critique group of romance and mystery writers signs at supermarkets that carry their books.
- A signing sponsored by The Romance Writers of America (http://www.rwanational.org/) benefits the Laubach Literacy Programs. A romance writer could join one of their efforts; authors in other genres could model this idea to suit their own needs.
- Use a charity event as an impetus to group signings. You, your fellow participants and your readers will recognize the extra value.
- Museums are possible venues. My first launch benefited the Gene Autry Museum of Western Heritage. They donated a well-equipped theater, promoted the event and allowed me to serve a buffet. The Museum kept 40 percent of the book sales as a donation. By the way, commercial bookstores do the same. The difference is that booksellers are a profitable venture rather than nonprofit.
- James Karlson, author of BLACK PETALS (www.jameskarlson.com), suggests matching non-traditional venues to the genre of your book. Mysteries at the police department as an example. Coffee houses and universities work well for a variety of books.
- My grandson's private school offered to sponsor a signing, as least in part because THIS IS THE PLACE is a coming of age story, but also because of our past support, I'm sure.

Handling Difficult Situations in Public

> A public man must never forget that he loses his
> usefulness when he as an individual, rather than his
> policy, becomes the issue.
> Richard M. Nixon

At book signings, readings or in interviews, authors may occasionally find themselves feeling defensive. We are now public persons and we must resist the urge to react. Take a deep breath and decide to treat the question or comment with respect. The person posing a pointed question may be tactless or ignorant and neither are reasons enough to be offended.

A fellow author who is subsidy published once e-mailed me this question, another Abigail Van Buren scenario:

> **Author:** Today I was at a book signing and during my question and answer period a man asked me rather rudely why someone with my credentials should choose to subsidy publish and mentioned that he had found typos in my book. In an interview earlier I was questioned about Jack Kelley's fabricated stories in USA today, as if I had something to do with them.

> **My Answer:** Try to give people like this a break; assume they just want information and talk about the industry in general. What's considered good about each form of publishing, what isn't. How the publishing industry, just like others, is not perfect. You might be armed with an anecdote of your own so that the heckler (if that is, indeed, what he is) is disarmed by your candor. Humor is helpful. On a similar occasion I told my questioner how the NY TIMES recently published a story accusing major publishers of inflating their first run figures for books in order to create buzz in the media and that compared to this kind of an...er...indiscretion, a typo or two hardly seems like a sin of great proportion. You might then turn the occasion into something positive by mentioning how your book or another published by your subsidy publisher was recently optioned for a movie or received a reward.

Sometime after such an upsetting moment we might examine our reaction to see what we can learn about ourselves, our writing or our choices. As an example we might consider if the reason we felt insulted lies within the realm of our own inadequacies.

During a book tour (yep, a real *tour*) in Georgia, I was confronted by a woman who asked if I knew the Mormon religion was a cult.

I have frequently encountered intolerance because I am *not* a Mormon. I handled the situation well enough (but not perfectly!), returning her question with a question about how she would define "cult." Nevertheless, the experience helped me see how deeply rooted the hurts I experienced as a child and teen-ager were, that I hadn't, in fact, "gotten over" them as I thought I had and, on the positive side, that I am offended as much by bigotry aimed at others as at myself. Self-examination helps authors handle encounters of the hard-to-take kind more effectively.

Tips for a Do-It-Yourself Book Tour

Adapt yourself to changing circumstances.
Chinese Proverbs

Even book tours that piggyback onto the needs of pleasure or business are expensive. If you want to do them well and do them on a budget, try these suggestions:

- Plan about six months in advance. You'll need a travel agent or be willing to juggle the travel arrangements yourself.
- Plan a tour of several books stores in the same city or region. Choose widely separated venues only if your other plans take you to each location.
- Choose independent bookstores when possible. Indies are more likely to be interested in your book, and will probably expend greater effort to promote your event. For best results, telephone a bookstore after you've queried them, if you can afford to do so.
- Get creative. Because THIS IS THE PLACE is set in the 50s and features a rusty '49 Buick convertible, I thought "touring" Route 66 in a classic car might be a good idea. The tour would be my vacation and it might be less costly that some other kind of vacation. It didn't pan out, but such a picture-perfect tour would surely have attracted enough publicity to make the effort (and expense?) worthwhile.
- Promote each signing and the tour as a whole. Use every trick in this book. Feature editors, the weekend calendar sections of the local newspaper, radio stations. Leave no pebble in place. Use a search engine to find organizations and media contacts.
- Plan tours in areas where you have a base of support or where there is special interest in your topic.

- Go on a tour well-equipped. That's hard when you fly, but it can be done. Expect the unexpected, even an unplanned radio interview or an opportunity to add another reading to your agenda.
- Let friends or relatives help. Choose a location where someone is willing to use her influence, invite her friends, lend you a car or a bed.
- Plan every aspect of the tour before you go. Consider canceling if the interest is not forthcoming.
- Record essentials in a special place in your travel journal or on a calendar you keep at your side. "Essentials" even include directions from your Motel 6 to the bookstore.
- When she is in a new city, Anne Holt, author of SILVER CREEK, www.ahholt.com, makes time to visit their libraries and other bookstores to drop off promotion packets. These might include an adaptation of your media kit, fliers, small posters to post on bulletin boards and a copy of your book if you can afford it.
- Meryl Zegarek, President of Meryl Zegarek Public Relations, Inc., suggests that authors who are receiving little positive response from bookstores guarantee sales of the books the bookstore purchases for the event. That means that if the store doesn't sell them within a given time, you or your publisher will buy them back. Negotiate. Ask if they will keep a certain number (usually 6) signed copies for 30 to 90 days. If they hesitate, offer to pay the return postage on them. Having said that, know that you may never see either the books or the money.

> Hint #1: I am not alone in preferring other methods of promoting books to signing them at bookstores. Francine Silverman, author of CATSKILLS ALIVE, also hates book signings. Learn more about her at www.bookpromotionnewsletter.com.

> Hint #2: If a publisher does your tour for you, take what you know about promotion beyond her efforts and soar!

Chapter 29: Book Fairs: Only As Good As You Make Them

...there are already beginning at present welcome dribbles (of profit) hitherward from the sales of my new edition, which I just job and sell, myself.
Walt Whitman

When authors assume book fairs are about sales rather than promotion they are setting themselves up for disappointment. Like many other sales-oriented promotions, book fairs are valuable sales tools only if you have a connection to the region or locale in which it is held. Here are examples:

- You live in San Bernardino, CA. The Inland Empire Bookfest would be perfect for you. Contact Ruth Day at: rday@sbccd.cc.ca.us.
- Your fiction is set in Los Angeles so the Los Angeles Times/ UCLA Book Fair might work.
- You have personal or business ties in Salt Lake City? Consider The Great Salt Lake Book Festival. Your contact is Jean Cheney at cheney@utahhumanities.org.
- A book about the idiosyncrasies of the dotcom industry might be a shoo-in at a Silicon Valley book fair.
- You are a featured guest and the book fair administration promotes you in their advertising campaign. Then you promote your own appearance to the local media. That kind of a slam-dunk might work anywhere.
- Intimate fairs are sometimes better for sales. New Yorkers will find The Small Press Book Fair a place where their star-shine will be more evident than at huge fairs. Learn more at http://www.smallpress.org.
- Choose a fair set up to benefit an organization. Lori Hein, author of RIBBONS OF HIGHWAY: A MOTHER-CHILD JOURNEY ACROSS AMERICA (www.lorihein.com) had excellent success at a book fair that benefited her daughter's

elementary school. She used signs to inform book fair revelers that $3 would be donated from every book sale and she sold 25 books. She says, "Two weeks later I'm still riding the coattails of that one book fair." She did a lot of things right:

- She chose a fair where she had personal ties.
- She chose a fair that was aligned to the title of her book. In other words, a school fair and a book about a parent-child relationship were a great team.
- She used good signs.
- She was specific about the amount she intended to donate.
- She passed out fliers and cards, complete with a good pitch and contact information. That is why she continued to sell books and get requests for other engagements after the fair.

However, book fairs are about more than selling books. They're about exposure. If you're self or subsidy published, you could get lucky and have a big publisher "find" you. A producer may come along, snag an obscure book from a booth and option it. Book fairs are opportunities to get your publicity balls polished and rolling like the silver spheres in a pinball machine.

No matter how you measure book fair success, here's how to give your book its best shot:

- Learn what the fair provides in the way of publicity, space and equipment.
- If there is a place in your booth, display a reusable banner, a great poster and signage that shouts out your awards.
- Be kind to your back. Take a roller board or a handcart.
- Get a gig at the fair reading or promoting in some way.
- Send media releases to the local press, TV, local libraries, bookstore event coordinators and buyers and book discussion group leaders. Include an angle and picture opportunity that will make you or your book irresistible to them.
- Send personal invitations to anyone you know in the area. Ask those you know who live there to invite their friends and offer to provide the fliers or invitations and pay the postage.
- Offer a special "fair-only discount" to interested readers.

- Wear a name tag that says "AUTHOR" in large letters. Use indelible ink on broad satin ribbon, clip it into a swallowtail shape and hang it from your name tag. Readers are impressed with authors; let them know you are one, even when you aren't in your booth.
- Try to find an entrée for your book in the booths of participating bookstores before the fair. If the Mystic Sisters Book Shop will have a booth, call their fair coordinator to see if she'll stock your book in the store's booth.
- Keep a guestbook; even if you don't sell a lot of books you'll be adding to your promotion power for your next book or next direct mail campaign.
- Partner with another author who will be there to share costs and cross promote.
- Give souvenir buttons to anyone who walks up to your booth. Don't just hand them out. Ask if you may pin them to your customers' shirts; they become your walking billboards and you'll make a friend.
- If someone from the press visits, don't just smile. *Ask* them for coverage. *Pitch* them ideas. *Help* them get the story they want.
- Be hospitable. Set out candy or snacks.
- If you'll be standing on the grass wear warm, comfy shoes, socks and bring a mat.
- Bring along a helper.
- Dress the part.
    - Literary authors could consider a scholarly look—perhaps a turtle neck and Harry Potter-style spectacles. Authors of children's books might wear a Disneyland-style costume.
    - Sassy T-shirts imprinted with your book cover work well for men and nonfiction authors (see chapter 13 under "Logo Items").
    - As a conversation starter, Kathleen Walls, author of GHOSTLY GETAWAYS, wears a bridal dress like the one on the cover of her book at some of the reenactments and events that have an antebellum connection.
- After the event, send pictures and a media announcement (see chapter three under "Editors Love Media Announcements").
- Be ready with positive, useful responses to sales resistance:

- If a browser says, "I already have too many books on my nightstand," the author says, "I know what you mean. However, if you know anyone who can use a presenter, I do those, too," as she hands them a card or flier.
- If a browser says, "I'm writing my own book, the author might say, "That's wonderful. I do editing," or "Maybe you'd like to sign up for my newsletter. I give tips in it for other authors! Here's the subscription information."

- Take a kit of essentials. Re-supply anything you run out of when you get back to home base.
- Pack a lunch. Even if you have a friend who can relieve you, you'll find that you are the star attraction. You are the one your visitors will want to talk to.
- Take sunscreen and a hat in case your awning doesn't arrive or in case the show doesn't provide them.
- Put on your best sales and promotion face. Stand, don't sit. Memorize a pitch and adapt it your audience (see the latter half of chapter two). "THIS IS THE PLACE is a coming-of-age story about a young woman about your age," worked for me for the younger crowd. I told the older ones how many awards it has won, including the Reviewer's Choice Award.
- Consider selling mugs or T-shirts imprinted with your book cover. If the weather turns foul, you might sell a lot of imprinted umbrellas or rain bonnets.
- Follow up on leads you collect as quickly as possible. Make notes in the moment on each business card about what you intend to do with it so you don't forget.
- Don't forget your thank you notes—to those who bought your book and to the fair coordinators. Maybe you couldn't be a presenter this time, but if you keep in touch, next time you might be the celebrity du jour.

Evaluate Your Experience

> Intellect evaluates evaluations, and looks for the meanings of situations as a whole.
> Richard Hofstadter, US historian

I often write quick evaluations of any kind of event in which I participate so I can refine the procedure for the next time 'round. Once my evaluations ferment, I can even assess my expectations, see how they misled me. I am including excerpts of one I wrote on one of the biggest and best, The LA Times Festival of Books (aaron.davis@latimes.com) after several acquaintances and I rented a booth under the banner of "Authors Coalition:"

"I'm tired, coming down off the Los Angeles Times/UCLA Fair. Advantages: Great fair. Tons of traffic. Festive fair-like atmosphere, seminars, talks, panels. Plenty of star quality— from the publishing kingdom and Hollywood. Two days is a perfect length of time. California upheld the exclusive contract I have with it for perfect weather.

"I rate this fair worthwhile: For exposure. For the experience. For inspiration from readers who think authors are wonderful. As a way to help other authors (there were plenty of them out and about on sunny Sunday).

"Disadvantages: This is a huge fair so there is tons of competition for every dollar spent. I didn't see many people carrying bags (watching this is a habit I developed when I owned retail stores). The price of the booth is high; it's highly unlikely an author will sell enough books to cover the fee, let alone make a profit. Next time consider sharing a booth with your publisher, dummy, or with one of the bookstores where you've done readings.

"Tally: In our booth the highest number of books sold in the two days was 45 (nonfiction). The lowest was 12 (fiction).

"I went to the school of experience. Here's what I learned. Before the event, ask about chairs. Try to have one for you and one for a friend. Our neighboring booth bought Staples' three-sided display boards used for science fairs this time of year. One of these would have been great for displaying reviews, blurbs, pictures, and book covers.

"Selling books: I didn't take enough change. My booth mates weren't armed with a policy regarding checks. Decide if you want to risk taking a bogus check or not. I decided I would because I'd rather have my book read and the risks are slight. It's better if you accept charges; rent a little charge machine and learn the ropes from your Visa provider."

Most of the suggestions I used earlier in this section were gleaned from these same notes. I also managed to write a poem from notes I took.

> Hint #1: If you come across a fair in your travels and wish you'd had a booth, wear an AUTHOR name tag as you browse. You'll be surprised at how many attendees will want to talk about your book. Keep the tag and a book with you at all times for just such an occasion.

> Hint #2: For information on how to design effective fliers, go to www.frugalfun.com/marketingtips.html. Scroll down to find Shel Horowitz's series on this subject. As you scroll you'll notice he has posted dozens of his articles on marketing.

Alternative Events

> The media uses the terms trade fairs and book fairs interchangeably. Its a conspiracy to confuse the uninitiated. Book fairs are open to the public, trade fairs admit only those who make, sell or buy books at wholesale.
> CHJ

An alternative to renting your own booth at a fair is to join an organization or find an independent agent and let them display your book at the fairs they attend. These organizations charge for this service but the amount is usually less than it would cost you to travel and rent a booth of your own. Try:

- Publishers Marketing Association (PMA) (www.pma-online.org/memben.cfm).
- Small Publishers Association of North America (SPAN) (www.spannet.org). Membership in this organization will benefit most authors, not just publishers or the self-published.
- Linda Friedman (bookevents@attbi.com) arranges for book signings and represents authors at other events.
- Contact local and state governments, libraries, school districts, business organizations, clubs, associations and bookstores for other kinds of events where you can set up displays. There are many possibilities but carefully consider how your book title fits into an event's target audience. As

an example, a book on classic cars might do well at an exhibit of classic cars on Main Street in Any Town, USA. A how-to crafts book is suited to craft fairs.
- Call the cities listed in -the front section of your phonebook and ask to be put on their mailing list. Tell them you are specifically interested in Parks & Recreation events.

Here is a list of sites where you will find hundreds of events of all kinds to promote your book:
- http://www.craftmasternews.com.
- http://abaa.org/pages/bookfairs/calendar2003.html.
- http://www.bookfairs.com/showlists.html.
- http://bestsellers.zezenetwork.com/bookfairs.shtml.
- http://lcweb.loc.gov/loc/cfbook/bookfair.html Click on the LOC's "Book Fairs and Other Literary Events."
- http://www.bellagiopublishingnetwork.org/events/bookfairs2003.htm.
- http://www.southfest.com/georgia.shtml.
- http://www.wordsmitten.com/cork.html.
- http://www.writersmonthly.com/.

Share and Cross-Promote Events

> Ahh, a dilemma nearly as poignant as Hamlet's. To share or not to share, that is the question.
> CHJ

Because you've been promoting you know other authors, maybe some with similar goals to yours. The benefits of sharing projects are:
- Sharing allows you to participate when the costs would otherwise be prohibitive.
- Until you have the confidence and expertise to go it alone, the support offered by others is invaluable.
- Cross-promotion can result in a better trafficked booth. Crowds draw still more people.

> Caveat: Choose partners whose book complements rather than detracts from yours. Be selective about your partners' reliability in terms of shared costs and shared promotional efforts.

Chapter 30: The Library's The Place

Help thi kynne, Crist bit (bids), for ther begynneth charite.

The author of PIERS THE PLOWMAN, approx. 1393

Make your library your showcase. Not only does your library need you, but if you choose libraries or some other reading and writing friendly organization, you will find support for your own projects that would be difficult to match elsewhere.

- Think of ways to contribute to your local library and others.
- Offer to lead a critique group.
- If they have a Friends of the Library program that features authors, query them for a spot on their agenda.
- Ask if they would feature your book in a display window or on a bulletin board. Volunteer time and supplies for the project.
- Let a good librarian help you with your list-building and other marketing efforts.
- Ask your librarian for leads when you research. You may be an expert on the subject but she is an expert on libraries.
- The authors of children's books could offer to read at the library's children's hour. Take small gifts for the children with an offer to sign a book if their parents should choose to buy one for them.
- When you help the library, make every effort to see that the library and you are given positive press within the community.

Chapter 31: Write Thank You Notes

A thank you note is not a duty, it is a return gift
Robin Spizman, the owner of The Spizman
Agency and author of more than 60 books

Your mother was only partially right. Of course you should write your thank you notes but you should also follow up on them for considerate behavior is the best kind of promotion.

Thank yous create good will. Good will creates opportunity. Carolyn See, the well-known California literary author of MAKING A LITERARY LIFE, suggests not only writing thank-you notes but also writing one "generous, lovely letter a day."

Here are four ways to let gratitude boost your promotion efforts and leave a little happiness in your wake:

- Write a sincere thank you when your book is reviewed, when you are interviewed, or when you are mentioned in a newsletter or article. Use your writing skill to make the recipient feel valued, not just a cursory note like the ones you tried to get away with when you were in the third grade.

   Hint: Your most memorable note will be the one you send to a reviewer who has been critical of your book. One of my least favorite reviews was written by Rebecca Brown at www.RebeccasReads.com. I told her—sincerely—that I learned much from her review and now my essays, letters-to-the-editors, rants, and more appear so regularly on her site she has made me an Associate Reviewer.

- Track the notes you send as part of your database. Include names, the dates you wrote, their e-mail, post and website addresses. Code your entry as to type of favor this person did for you (i.e. interview, review) and for which of your books. If this is your first book it won't be long before there will be another and you'll want to have a complete record for your next query or thank you.

- Follow up. Two weeks after a review, check out this person's website or newsletter. You're looking for some other way you might help her. Offer to contribute to her newsletter. Send her a gift or offer her a copy of your book for a contest she runs on her site.

- When you publish another book or have some other writing news that may fit with this particular editor or reviewer's scope of interest, you will be remembered. Mention how you and that editor are connected when you send the query about your new idea. You'll be on your way to more publicity and a still firmer relationship.

Notes make friends because your authenticity shows. From a practical standpoint you can help a contact when she needs a tip sheet or article and she will be interested in your news. When this endeavor is multiplied many times over you'll also have a permanent, personal, reusable publicity list, one that is better than most professional publicists could offer you.

Closely aligned with thank yous are other niceties, like asking editors if this is a convenient time to talk, offering collateral material to "make their job easier," including alternate contact information and anything else that brands you as efficient and caring.

> Hint #1: A snapshot taken at an event that includes poses of the person you're thanking may be a more thoughtful addition to your note than something more costly.

> Hint #2: When media friends receive awards, redesign their pages, write a great feature story or are assigned a new column, send them congratulatory notes. Learn about these successes by reading the editor's column at the beginning of magazines and by reading what she writes.

Chapter 32: Amazon Offers Perks: Use Them to Your Advantage

The mightiest river in the world is the Amazon. It runs from west to east, from the sunset to the sunrise, from the Andes to the Atlantic.

Theodore Roosevelt

Among authors, Amazon.com has earned its name. For many it is their most important tool for online sales; sometimes it is their not-so-gentle giant. It is a business many love to hate. Several of its policies are perceived to be anti-author. Because it has so many features that are an advantage to authors, I, instead, hate to admit that I love it.

Amazon Sells

Ahhhh, Amazon. When it comes to book sales, she strides on the sturdiest of legs.

CHJ

Amazon, like the great woman warrior of mythology, performs amazing feats. She will sell your books here and overseas. She may not cater to authors of any stripe, but she tolerates them as long as they are assigned an ISBN (the number on the back of your book near the barcode). Small or large publishers, subsidy, and self-published books may be found in her pages making her a unique buying and selling tool. She also offers—with an outstretched hand and only a few guidelines—avenues that will expose your book to a very important target, *readers.* Because Amazon is fickle—always adding a feature or taking something away, always changing page designs, I can only attempt to give exact instructions for implementing the features she offers. It is important for you to sign in so that a little index tab sporting your name pops up on the home page. Mine says "Carolyn's Store."

Yours will be equally well personalized once you are a customer. Click on that tab for a myriad of possibilities for your book.

Amazon's "Your About You Page"
Adapt yourself to changing circumstances
Chinese Proverb

Once you are an author you must forget the adage "Fools' names and fools' faces are always seen in public places." You seize an opportunity like Amazon's "Your About You Area" to expose yourself and your book to readers. This "area" on Amazon.com is a page—much like a website of your own—that you can tailor to appeal to readers surfing for something to read. When a visitor to Amazon finds your book, the reviews, essays, and recommended reading lists you have posted on the site, they will also find a link to this page where they can read more about you—not necessarily the private you, but the author you. Because these perks reach your targeted audience—readers—and because they cost you nothing but time, they are a bargain. Make them part of your promotion strategy. Here's how you post your page:

- Go to www.amazon.com.
- Find the tabs near the headline. You've signed in with Amazon so you'll find a personalized tab at the top of the page. Click.
- Find "Your About You Area" on the left side of page under "Communities." Click.
- Install a page in "Your About You Area." Add your picture or book cover art. Use a short synopsis of your book as part of your biography.
- While you're there, explore this area. There are many features here that might interest you. I have listed my favorites below.

Amazon's "So You'd Like To...Guide"
...be candid where we can...
Alexander Pope

Amazon's "So You'd Like To..." is a feature where you can post articles, essays, rills or rants on any subject that you wish. At the bottom of the article you type in the ISBN numbers (but Amazon calls them ASIN numbers) of books or other products related to the subject of your piece. Readers who visit the pages of the books you listed may then find your article available to read.

"So You'd Like To...Guides" are an excellent place to recycle your old articles (see chapter 32—a subhead is devoted to these guides) because the interest of readers is as wide as the world and beyond. That means pretty much anything you still own the rights to can be posted here to be read by book-lovers. Edit the material so it relates to your book in some way. This connection is the primary reason for "giving" an essay to Amazon.

Here are some tips for contributing a successful "So You'd Like To":

- Find the "So You'd Like To...." link on "Your About You Page."
- Read the instructions and guidelines at the top of the page.
- Come up with a title that invites browsers to read it. One of mine that has attracted heavy readership is "So You'd Like To... Know More About Elizabeth Smart's Culture." Every time Elizabeth's court case (she's the teen-ager who was kidnapped by a radical self-styled prophet in Utah) makes the news, this essay gets another spurt of curious readers.
- Copy and paste your article into the text window.
- Carefully edit. Amazon's free offer deserves to be honored with your best. Besides, your reputation as a writer is on the line.
- At the end, type in up to 50 related book, tape, and video titles according to the instructions. I used the book written by Elizabeth's parents and others on facets of Utah's culture including its renegade polygamist cells.
- Include some books on your list that will attract heavy traffic from book-lovers. That helps exposure. Longer lists are spotted throughout Amazon more often than short ones.
- Use my "So You'd Like To...Guides" as examples by going to: http://www.amazon.com/exec/obidos/tg/cm/member-guides/-/A3JH18T58CY65P/ref=cm_aya_bb_sylt/102-3003008-8964967. So far I have 17 of them and each day they attract more readers.
- Include the title of your book in the body of the essay. If you have chosen your subject carefully your book will be a natural fit.
- Click on the "publish" button when you're done.
- You may begin with a short list and add to it using the edit feature.

- Voila! This list will magically appear on many pages throughout the Amazon site. It will be targeted primarily to the books that you chose to list but may appear elsewhere.

I recently started helping authors I know by offering to include their books on one of the "So You'd Like To..." lists. I recycled (and rewrote) one of the "Back to Literature" columns I had published at www.myshelf.com. It was an opinion piece on how important it is for authors to be accessible to their fans. Then I posted an offer to fellow authors who share a list-serve with me. I told them what I was doing and asked for volunteers. I also asked them to promise me they would be accessible to fans by offering a gift or a signature label to them if they were contacted. I had to turn away so many grateful authors who wanted to be included that I'm planning another article as soon as I figure out a new angle to help the other authors and give the right kind of exposure to my books. Here is the link for that essay: http://www.amazon.com/exec/obidos/tg/guides/guide-display/-/H3M5DP3WRXDS/ref=cm_bg_dp_1_2/102-2927160-6432116. Some of my SYLTs have made it to Amazon's top 100, but I haven't figured out the criteria they use or why they seem to rotate on and off the list, and I can't find anyone else who has figured it out either.

Building Amazon "Listmanias"

> Lists are like tulip bulbs, they proliferate with hardly any effort once theyve been planted.
> CHJ

"Listmania" is a feature provided by Amazon to its visitors to list products or books that they feel are exemplary. "Listmanias" are built much like the "So You'd Like To...Guides", but with less work. For "Listmanias" you need only write brief blurbs about each book you post because Amazon has streamlined the process of finding the ISBNs for your entries. I expect they'll eventually get around to installing a similar system on their "So You'd Like Tos..."

Each individual "Listmania" does not, however, attract the readership of SYLTs. Amazon tracks readership (and ratings) for you so it's easy to see exactly how many hits each of your efforts attracts.

As an author, you read and know books well. Think of how your book fits into any number of topics and compile a "Listmania" for each. Here's how:

- Go to www.amazon.com.
- Find the tabs near the headline. Find the personalized one. If yours doesn't appear, you'll need to sign in first. Click.
- Go to "Friends and Favorites" on the right side of page. Click.
- Find the "Listmania" link. Click.
- Be prepared with at least three books you want to list in any category you've chosen. Don't list yours first. Amazon discourages that because it's the cover of the first listed book that appears with your Listmania title. Amazon is luke warm to authors promoting their own books, probably because some take advantage.
- Each list accepts up to 25 titles.
- You add a mini-review (up to two lines) for each book you list.
- In the window provided for credentials, list those that will contribute to your branding efforts.
- Doing "Listmanias" is like branding or building presence on a search engine. Frequency counts.
- Like anything, baby steps can eventually take you a mile. Start small. Keep working at it.
- Explore ideas for how to relate your "Listmanias" to your book by checking out how I did it for my lists: http://www.amazon.com/exec/obidos/tg/cm/member-fil/-/A3JH18T58CY65P/ref=cm_hp_stats_list-count/103-2121127-5313447. Don't be discouraged by the number of lists I've done; I've been working at it with a publicist's vengeance for at least a year.

Voting on Amazon

> The fact that a man is to vote forces him to think.
> John Jay Chapman, US author

Almost every contribution on Amazon can be rated with up to five stars. That includes all of the features discussed in this book and more. If you do a review, ask the author of the book to take the time to rate your review. You do the same for others. Karma, karma, karma.

Voting can be tricky. Kam Ruble, award-winning novelist and poet, was perusing my "Listmania" lists and was confused: "The first time I went to vote, I didn't realize one had to click on a star, I just kept sliding my cursor and getting nowhere," she says. She is probably right, when she says, "If I couldn't figure it out, just think how many others can't either."

This is how you vote for a "Listmania." You are browsing through Amazon and notice a "Listmania" (they're on the right hand side of a book's page). When you click on it, you will find a string of five faded stars somewhere near the top of the list. You point at the highest star rating you want to give the list and then click. A "thank you for your vote" message appears. That is your assurance that your rating has taken like a well-intentioned vaccination. The voting mechanism is slightly different on each of Amazon's features, but once you've figured one, the others are easier.

There is also a feature on each "Listmania" that allows you to e-mail the list to a friend. Do so, asking the friend to rate your list if they like it. It is also a good idea to e-mail the authors whose books you have listed. It creates good will for you, cooperation among authors and increases traffic for Amazon. Do them the favor. They, after all, have extended this opportunity to you.

Amazon and Other Web Booksellers' Ratings

Confusion is a word we have invented for an order which is not understood.

Henry Miller, US author

Once authors know about the online booksellers' ratings they often make a big deal over them but I don't know a single person who understands what they mean or how they work. I wouldn't be surprised if Jeff Bezos, founder and CEO of Amazon, couldn't explain the method they use; it is more mysterious and far less publicized than Einstein's formula for the theory of relativity.

You will hear so many different opinions on how the sites assign the ratings and how to rig them that it will make you dizzy. If you let them, ratings will take your mind off your writing and promoting.

Don't try to beat the booksellers' ratings game. David Vise, author of THE BUREAU AND THE MOLE, got some publicity for allegedly trying to rig the NEW YORK TIMES' bestseller list by buying up huge numbers of books; don't concern yourself with emulating his "success." It probably won't work a second time. Others have tried contests or free offers to manipulate huge one-day sales on Amazon in order to make their book a "bestseller." That, too, has been done and is recognized by all as a gimmick.

The only practical use for this rating may be that an author can judge when her book's sales have slowed down on one particular bookseller's site. On Amazon you find this rating in the section that includes your publisher's name; it's near the top of the page your book appears on.

I check my rating only on Amazon and then only occasionally. It is the only one that is meaningful because I refer those who want to order my book to that site. They offer all the perks I've mentioned in this section so it seems only fair to send them my business and it simplifies the rating game for me.

When you notice your rating declining, renew your promotion efforts. Come back to this book, review it, and choose a new tack to spur sales. When you're trying to figure out Amazon's rating system, remember, the lower your rating's number, the better the news.

If you prefer to track your ratings more avidly, you may want to subscribe to a time-saving service at: www.booksandwriters.com.

Amazon's "What's Your Advice"

> ...such a flourishing train of attendants will give your book a fashionable air, and recommend it for sale.
> Miguel de Cervantes, from DON QUIXOTE

Amazon's "What's your Advice" feature allows readers to recommend books to one another just as they would if they were invited to a salon where the conversation might go:

> "Oh, you like books about tolerance?"

> "I was intrigued with how FIRST THE RAVEN exposed the secular Jewish community's intolerance for the more traditional forms of Judaism."

The idea is to give prospective readers a lead on a similar book, just as you would in conversation with a fellow reader.

When Amazon first introduced this feature it was abused by one author who used it to recommend her own book on hundreds and hundreds of best selling books' pages without consideration for theme or similarities of any kind. Her enthusiasm was noted in major media (it is possible that she alerted them herself), and though the author was one who came with high credentials, the publicity was all negative. Nevertheless, she felt it was worthwhile. No matter what your ethical take on this kind of exposure might be, this ploy has been used and won't work twice. Besides, it is my theory that the universe smiles on those who are kind to the system.

I first heard about "What's Your Advice" from Annette Gisby, author of SHADOW OF THE ROSE (www.twistedtales.n3.net). She suggests that authors who use this feature should put their recommendation in the "in addition to" box, not the "instead of." It seems a matter of courtesy to other authors. Flower, the skunk in Disney's BAMBI, tells us, "If you can't say something nice, don't say anything at all."

Other suggestions for using this feature:
- Have the ISBN number (the number on the barcode on the back of each book) of the book you are recommending handy.
- Be sure that the book you suggest relates in a substantial way to the book appearing on that page.
- Take care to recommend only books that are listed on Amazon. If they aren't, your suggestions will not "take."
- Ask others to recommend your book using this feature.

Amazon Reviews

A critic is a man who expects miracles.
James Gibbons Huneker, from ICONOCLASTS

As an author you are an avid reader anyway; it only takes a few moments to add a thoughtful review on Amazon and other readers' sites like BN.com that allow these voluntary posts.
- See chapter four under "Write Reviews" on how to use your reviews to brand your name.

- Click on Amazon's link that gives review guidelines. There is no point in wasting your time because of a minor infraction.
- Use a jazzy or thought-provoking title for your review.
- Type in your byline before you start your review.
- Type in a brief tagline at the end of your review but, unlike other sites, do *not* use your website address in it. Your review will be rejected if you use a website address—yours or any other.
- When you have that personalized tab on the home page of Amazon, your review will automatically include a link to that lovely little Amazon feature, "Your About You Area."
- Edit your review. Copy, paste, rewrite and add one to BN.com as well.
- Amazon readers are more likely to click to learn more about you or your book if your Amazon reviews are attention grabbers.
- When possible, let the author know that you posted a review of her book on Amazon. It's more than a courtesy. She will feel honored.
- If you cannot recommend a book, consider not posting. That doesn't mean, of course, that we must post only rave reviews nor that noting weaknesses aren't valid. It's just that there is no point in slashing and burning a book an author has invested herself in.

Do Unto Others

> Who will not mercie unto others show, How can he mercy ever hope to have?
>
> Edmund Spenser, from FAIERIE QUEENE

We must choose our own ethical path when promoting on Amazon, the Web at large or anywhere else. There are many self-appointed watch dogs who make an effort to see that the Amazon system is not abused. One is a gentleman who politely ignored my request for his name. His address is amazonvotewatch@yahoo.com; you might contact him for what he considers abuse of the system. Some Amazon personnel also patrol these features.

I am more relaxed about the guidelines that surround Amazon's perks than some and more conservative than many. Authors and publishers are naturally more interested in books than many others and so it is logical that they will be among those who employ these nifty features. I believe that because authors and publishers have a vested interest in books, they will be careful about how they utilize free speech to both rate others' participation and to review other authors' works. I believe that it is legitimate to ask for ratings but not appropriate to advocate a particular rating. I believe that Amazon's features should be used to promote readership in general thereby helping to increase the sales of this corporate giant that provides these opportunities. Let's all treat the system gently so it will treat us well in return.

Other Features

> Learning Amazons features is like climbing a trellis where thorns grow among the roses.
> CHJ

Amazon is constantly introducing new features and tinkering with the ones they offer. It is your job to find the ones that best suit your style, your book, your promotional needs, and then take baby steps to get started.

Amazon's "Top Reviewers" list is an all-star list for reviewers who post to their site. Reaching for this hallowed ground may be an impossible goal because of several reviewers who must spend every waking hour reading and writing about books. Harriet Klausner is the top reviewer and has reviewed nearly 7,000 books. You, I'm sure, would rather write another novel or have a root canal than try to beat that record.

Amazon's "My Amazon Friends" helps you build an e-mail list. I haven't used it though I have people on my list that I've added as a courtesy when they placed my name on their "friends" list but it could be useful for notifying friends and getting discounts or credits against your book purchases.

Amazon as search engine is a concept novel enough for TIME magazine to report on. It allows researchers to find your book not only by title and author but also by phrases in the content of the book. As an example, if you have a paragraph on any page in your book that mimics the key words in someone's search, you book will be listed. Thus, when you search on "This is the Place," my book appears among thousands in which that phrase or its individual words are used somewhere in their texts.

Amazon's "Advantage" is a feature that lets any independent publisher or author post their book to Amazon. Unlike other services, there is a fee for this. Most subsidy publishers and traditional publishers provide this listing service to their authors but if yours doesn't, find the link to this program at the left of the home page screen.

Manage your book's Amazon page. Add excerpts from reviews that praise your book. The link http://www.amazon.com/exec/obidos/subst/partners/publishers/list-titles.html/103-9731180-0051823 will give you the guidelines for "fair use" of copyright. You'll learn how many words you may use from someone else's work—in this case a review—without getting permission and how to credit the journal. Nina Osier, author of ROUGH RIDER (http://www.geocities.com/nina_osier/): suggests we use this link to add anything your publisher may have left out of the book's description or to fix errors. Use the link labeled "Content."

Amazon's "New and Used" feature lets you sell slightly damaged and return books and excess ARCs with Amazon. Go to your page and find the link at the top of the page near the availability entry. When that page comes up a "Sell Yours Here" tab will guide you through the process.

Common Misconception

> ...report not things which he had learned of others only by hearsay, but which he had with his own eyes presently seen and thoroughly viewed...
> Sir Thomas More, from UTOPIA

If you haven't already heard, the gossip mills churned out by authors who naturally love to talk will soon notify you that the work you post to Amazon becomes their property and cannot be published elsewhere.

I asked Amazon's customer service about their claim to "own" material posted there. Their answer makes it clear that they own only the right to "reuse" what you post there but that the author may continue to use the material as she sees fit. Some may not be pleased that about Amazon's using their work as they "see fit," but if an author chooses to post on Amazon, it is available for other uses by the writer.

This comes directly from Amazon's customer service department:

> "When a customer posts a 'So You'd Like to... Guide' to our site, the customer is granting us the nonexclusive right to use the guide. This means that once a guide is submitted to our site, the guide is ours to use as we see fit for as long as we wish. As this license is non-exclusive, the customer who has written the guide can also use the guide as he or she sees fit. The guide can be included in a book or posted on another site."
>
> Nicole L., Amazon.com Customer Service, http://www.amazon.com

Another common misconception is that efforts like those I've described here do not result in sales. Alan Fisk, author of CUPID AND THE SILENT GODDESS (http://www.twentyfirstcenturypublishers.com/index.asp?PageID=496) gave me permission to use him as my example that they do. He is one of many who saw one of my Amazon Listmania lists and followed the links to find me. It is often difficult to trace one's public relations efforts; it is cause to celebrate when we get proof as indelible as the ink in broad, black marker pens that our effort worked.

Chapter 33: Using Free and Low Cost E-Books To Promote

E-books may not be news to writers but they are still the darlings of the media. Exploit this love affair by sending them a Valentine.
CHJ

There may be as many different kinds of electronic books as you're likely to find of the more substantial kind in bookstores. There you see hardcover books, trade paperbacks, mass market paperbacks, books bound with twirly wires, pop-up books, large-print books, tactile books and more. E-books are all electronic but they come in all sizes from white papers that should, by all rights, be called e-papers—not e-books—to full-blown 360 page how-to books. They are given away and sold, usually inexpensively. They are offered as .pdf files, ready for readers to read on their screens or to be printed out and read the old-fashioned way and those that can be downloaded to multimedia readers for reading on the run. Surely one of them can be used to your advantage.

Once you have utilized this technology let the press know about it. That I am publishing an e-book may be greater interest in the general press than the more narrow angle of marketing for writers because all things tekky fascinate the general population, books on writing are more narrowly targeted.

Spur Stale Book Sales with an E-Book

An e-book format can breathe oxygen into a book that is about to expire.
CHJ

"Never say never," is an adage I ascribe to but have ignored for way too many years. E-books are my latest reminder that I am a slow learner.

My first take on e-books was that they can't be held or smelled or slid from a shelf. I sniffed in disgust. "What, no dusty fingers? No deliciously tattered dust covers? No turned-back corners and margin notes?"

In my mind, the books you could "have and hold until death do us part" were the only authentic books. I simply could not get over attitudes sculpted in granite decades before that "e" was not a prefix for anything, but especially not a book. I had published two "real" books in three years, gained a lot of experience in the new world of publishing and lots of expertise in promoting.

Obviously e-books could not have any real value if they couldn't offer even one of the tangible benefits I valued. My stupidity was showing. Soon I learned how valuable e-books can be for promoting one's "real" books. With several other authors I collaborated on three e-books, COOKING BY THE BOOK, SEASONED GREETINGS and MUSINGS: AUTHORS DO IT WRITE! But more about that in the next section of this chapter.

That these efforts at promotion with e-books were so successful should have opened my mind to all the e-book possibilities. The limitations of traditional publishing should have also nudged me into becoming a fan of e-books. One of those limitations is that regular books published by traditional presses go out of print so quickly. The shelf life of a carton of pasteurized milk can be longer than the time a bookstore will give a new author to prove herself. I learned this when Waldenbooks, a chain that had been very good to me by sponsoring more than 30 of my book signings, gave me the jolting news: I had contacted one of them to see if they still had some copies of THIS IS THE PLACE because I would be interviewed about Utah and the Elizabeth Smart case on a morning radio station in their area. "No, we're out," the voice on the phone said.

"If you'll order a few more of them, I could mention your store during the radio interview."

"Oh, I'm sorry, but we don't order any books over 90 days old."

I was astounded. Too stunned to note that I must, then, be in very good company and that their stores must be very short on titles by Dickens and Dostoevsky as well as Howard-Johnson.

Some time after that, my publisher came to my rescue. They started a new "E-Library" featuring their best-selling titles and both of mine were among them. Imagine that. New life for two books that—just like people and fine wine—don't get older, only better.

Because of this new turn of events:

- Both THIS IS THE PLACE and HARKENING are now available as e-books for only $5.95. That should make them accessible to a whole cadre of readers who loathe paying bookstore prices.
- My publisher is promoting their new e-book library and my books should receive some residual benefits. (Please notice I didn't say they are promoting my books, only the new library and contents therein. An author can only hope for so much!)
- I can use this new publishing event to query radio, TV and newspaper contacts I made early on, for now I have new fuel for the PR mill.

> Caveat: If your book is traditionally published, pitch the e-book idea to your publisher. Back up your pitch with a kick-butt marketing plan. If they aren't set up to publish e-books you can wait until your contract has expired and do it yourself.

I can't promise I'll "never say never again," but I'm certain that when I do (I told you I was a slow learner), those words will not be used in conjunction with e-anything but especially not e-books. I am a convert, pure and simple. Thus, you may be reading THE FRUGAL BOOK PROMOTER as an e-book. My reasons are many:

- I can offer it inexpensively to both accomplished and starving authors.
- Once written I was able to have it ready to use as a syllabus of sorts for my UCLA Writers' Program classes in as little as 30 days.
- I can alter it reasonably easily to keep it up to date.
- The number of pages is not an issue; I can include whatever I feel my readers—my fellow authors—will need.

Using Free E-Books to Promote

The widespread offering of gifts as part of product promotions has given the *free gift* a meaning all its own

THE AMERICAN HERITAGE BOOK OF ENGLISH USAGE

The new math for free publicity is: E-book + E-gift = Promotion. Oops. Error. Make the answer FREE promotion.

My best promotion accidentally fell into my lap. It is a free e-book called COOKING BY THE BOOK. There are three magical concepts in this paragraph:

1. Accidental.
2. Free.
3. E-book.

I'll share more about these three promotional potions a bit later.

COOKING BY THE BOOK is a concept developed by Kathleen Walls, www.globalauthorspublications.com. She asked more than two dozen authors from several countries to contribute to an e-book that would be given away free to anyone. It could be used as a gift of appreciation to the support teams it takes to edit and market a book and to the legions of readers who cook but who had never read any of our "real" books.

Only authors who had included at least one kitchen scene in her book were invited to contribute to COOKING BY THE BOOK. Each segment of the cookbook begins with an excerpt from that scene, the recipe comes next and then there is a short blurb about the author. We believed—if there is anything new in the world— that we had come up with a whole new cookbook concept. We knew that we had created an outstanding promotional tool.

This e-tool was a cross-pollinator. Each contributing author was to publicize it any way she chose. The only caveats were that participants must not charge for our joint effort and they must promote it. That way each contributor benefited from the efforts, the lists, and the contacts of the other authors. It turned out that we had some superior promoters among us:

- Joyce Livingston set up a promotional page for the cookbook on the site she uses to promote ALASKAN MIDNIGHT (www.joycelivingston.com); most of the other authors followed suit.
- Contributor Peggy Hazelwood promoted it in her newsletter for book lovers and writers, the Albooktross Web-foot News.
- Mary Emma Allen writes novels and nonfiction but she's also featured the cookbook in the columns she writes for New Hampshire dailies THE CITIZEN and THE UNION LEADER.
- David Leonhardt, (http://thehappyguy.com/) author of CLIMB YOUR STAIRWAY TO HEAVEN, incorporated the cookbook into a Happiness Game Show speech that he delivered over a dozen times in Canada and elsewhere.
- We all gave away coupons offering this gift at book signings. Because it costs nothing, it is a gift that can be given to everyone, not just those who purchase a book. Some had bookmarks made up featuring this offer.
- True to form, I did a lot of cheerleading. I redesigned my business cards to a two-sided affair with an "e-gift" offer on the back. I think the "thank you" aspect of a promotional e-book is one of the most valuable ways they can be used.

Reviewer JayCe Crawford (http://www.authorsden.com/jaycecrawford) said, "For a foodie-*cum*-fiction-freak like me, this cookbook is a dream come true." That review has popped in places we didn't even know existed. One finds these pleasant promotion surprises by surfing the search engines using your book's title or other entities related to the book like the reviewer's name. You may be surprised at how many needles of this sort you can find in the Web haystack.

Our most startling success came from sources we had no connection to at all. It was featured in Joan Stewart's THE PUBLICITY HOUND, in WRITER'S WEEKLY, in the iUniverse newsletter and more.

When I queried radio stations for interviews with angles related to this cookbook, I had the highest rate of response I'd ever had and that was in competition with a pitch for THIS IS THE PLACE just before the 2002 games in Salt Lake City and an intolerance angle on the same novel right after 9/11.

I'm not through promoting this book yet. Mother's day is an occasion that beckons each of us to repeat our publicity blitzes every year, because, if you haven't noticed, mothers tend to do lots of cooking. This book was so successful I collaborated with Sarah Mankowski (www.bookbanter.com) on a similar one called SEASONED GREETINGS for the holidays and then switched gears slightly and worked with Kristie Leigh Maguire on an inspirational book for writers called MUSINGS: AUTHORS DO IT WRITE!

Back to those three magic words:
1. **Accidental:** I don't take credit for knowing a good thing when I see it. What I learned from this experience is to never dismiss something that is placed on your desk without careful consideration—even if it seems vaguely hokey. I nearly did just that. "E-book indeed," I said under my breath. I was worried that association with this concept might taint my work of literary art. Hubris can be self-defeating.
2. **Free**: This charmed word often convinced editors to present our cookbook as a freebie to their visitors and readers. Many websites featured it on their home pages. Usually the contributing author who pitched an idea was privileged with their own promotional site's URL being used as a link, thus motivating those authors who hadn't publicized as actively as others to do more. Some editors chose to place the entire cookbook download on their own site rather than provide a link, and that was OK, too.
3. **E-book**: This concept is important because an e-book is easy for people to obtain and can be offered free by the author. She need not budget for postage or processing expenses. In the invitations, queries, and releases I sent out, I emphasized a "no strings attached" policy: I didn't ask that they register at my site, sign up for a newsletter nor purchase a thing. The E-book concept is also important because it can be the hook for obtaining an article or an interview.

Oh, and there may be a fourth magic word. *Cookbook*. Our group of authors found this word had universal appeal. You might find something that ties in better with what you're doing. I've been thinking of doing a book about genealogy because my novel is based on the stories of my own ancestors, four generations of them.

It is not necessary that the freebie be knitted to your primary title; you may benefit by a theme that reaches out to draw in those who might not otherwise be exposed to your work. These ideas may appeal to a narrower audience than a cookbook but it will still appeal to those who love something that is FREE.

Here are some ways I promoted these e-books:
- I give them as gifts, or in this case, e-gifts.
- I use them as thank yous to people who visit my site.
- I pass out coupons offering them at events. I want to encourage both those who buy my books and those who don't to visit my site.
- I include information on these gifts on the back of my business cards for the same reasons.
- I send out my news releases on these books whenever I run across another place that seems as if one of them would interest their audience.

COOKING BY THE BOOK and my other e-books are like hospitality gifts only better. They promote not only my work but that of others. (If the concept interests you, go to http://carolynhowardjohnson.com to download them.)

Here is more reading on the subject of e-books:
- http://www.ebooks-made-easy.com/viralbook.
- Sign up for Dirk Dupon's newsletter at smartpromotion-subscribe@topica.com.
- Download Cathi Stevensen's free e-book, BUDGET BOOK PROMOTION, that gives lots of online hotspots for promoting e-books and others: http://www.bookcoverarttemplates.com/

> Hint #1: You might also offer a free book or smaller e-paper, e-storybook or e-novella as a free gift with the purchase of your regular book.

> Hint #2: You could send out an offer for a free book of spiritual poems or stories or even a brief nonfiction book on the history of the holidays with your seasonal greeting card. Your friends and relatives might spend an additional few minutes during the holidays with you—on your site.

Chapter 34: Catalog Sales Are Exposure, Too!

> Catalogs are show business. They spotlight a product for the sole purpose of selling merchandise but they also create a buzz, project an image, tell a story, leave an impression. They create celebrity for themselves and for each of their products.
> CHJ

Experts disagree about how extensive the crossover is between sales and publicity. The primary reason for your book to appear on the pages of a retail catalog is, of course, sales but that exposure is also extraordinary publicity for your book.

It qualifies as publicity because you don't pay for it. It is paid advertising for the catalog company or store that issues the catalog; for you it is a free ride that will result not only in sales through the catalog itself but will stir up interest in all kinds of other places.

Other advantages are:
- The catalog company will probably pay the freight for their book shipments.
- Their purchases are outright; unlike most bookstores, they will not return what they buy.
- They will reorder when their stock is depleted.
- They don't care if your book is current as long as the information is accurate and it sells.
- Most don't require exclusivity.
- Their orders will be substantial enough to make both you and your publisher smile. That your publisher probably will not attempt to sell your books this way is beyond understanding, but they probably won't.

Disadvantages are:

- Learning curve ahead! You'll need to negotiate sales to catalog buyers expertly.
- Because catalogs buy in quantity they may expect a hefty discount. If you or your publisher cannot give 50 percent or more, there is no point in pursuing this avenue. However, if you only break even on catalog sales, it may be worth pursuing them for the publicity benefits.
- Some authors and publishers fail to print enough books to supply a catalog's needs.
- Nonfiction books are generally more suitable for catalogs.

Here's how to find catalogs that might be interested in your book:

- Do an engine search on "retail catalogs." About 600,000 lists and individual catalogs will appear. Narrow the search to include only catalogs that will find your book irresistible.
- Go to a bookstore or library for CATALOG OF CATALOGS. Find one or more categories that are a fit for your book and Bibbidi, Bobbidi, Boo! Another way to see your book cover in print and realize sales at the same time.
- The fast but more expensive way to find leads is to purchase John Kremer's specialty retailer and catalog databases for about $60 from www.bookmarket.com/orderform.html.
- Watch for catalogs that come to your home. Become familiar with their products. Ask your friends to pass their catalogs on to you. When you find an appropriate one for your book, go for it!
- Read BEYOND THE BOOKSTORE by Brian Jud. Call (800)-43-BRIGHT.

> Hint: It is almost a certainty that your publisher won't pursue this avenue for sales. If you can crack a catalog deal for a gross or more of your title, it is highly unlikely that your publisher won't see the value in it and work with you. If you approach your publisher first, they most probably won't be up for it. They may not understand the potential until it is laid in their laps.

Chapter 35: Corporate Sales

Many companies give presents to clients...such gifts should be kept inexpensive enough so they are not seen as bribes.

Amy Vanderbilt, from THE AMY VANDERBILT COMPLETE BOOK OF ETIQUETTE

In addition to gifts for social occasions and holidays, large and small companies also give gifts to their employees as awards or perks. Sometimes they have training programs (yes, think books!) that help teach their employees and clients subjects they deem vital to their success. Generally they buy in quantity and expect discounts from regular retail prices. Here are some ways to pursue these sales if your book fits the needs of any particular industry.

- Once again, you'll need to get creative. How does the subject of your book align with a specific business or industry? How might you convince a corporation that it would benefit from utilizing your book?
- If you know someone in a corporation that is a "match" for you book, ask for their recommendation. Send a thank you even if your collaboration doesn't work out.
- Set up your own site and use sites like www.findgift.com to help business administrators find you.
- If you're self-published you might think of a way that your book could be personalized to meet the needs of large corporations. As an example, this one might be titled John Wiley & Sons' Primer: How Our Authors Might Contribute to the Success of Their Own Books. I would have to edit out the parts that make publishers look less than promotion minded—especially if they liked this idea enough to do it. A special introductory or dedication page might also personalize a book for corporate use.

- Contact Jerry Jenkins at www.specialmarketbooksales.com for ideas and services for special market book sales. Or call (800)-706-4636.

> Caveat: Corporate sales usually only work well for "gift" books, cookbooks and books with a business theme. Fiction is a hard sell. However, if a novelist comes up with an idea that she believes in, it can never hurt to present it.

Chapter 36: Retail Is More than Bookstores

Books arent the sole purview of bookstores any more. A title may fit into the merchandise mix of some kind of retailer—from a tire store to a fast food chain.

CHJ, from a gift trade show seminar

In recent years, a category called "gift books" has become a hot commodity in retail circles. Almost any store can sell a book that is closely aligned with its image and its customers' needs.

Retail sales are one more building block in your publicity blitz. Exposure in retail establishments creates demand at libraries and bookstores. This is especially useful long after the shelf life on a new release has supposedly expired and bookstores have lost interest.

Start selling to gift and other retail stores in your community. Unless your publisher is one that specializes in gift books, they probably won't approach retailers other than booksellers, but you can make traditional sales calls to local retailers without them.

If you are convinced that a particular store could sell a ton of your books use what is called a "forced sale" technique. Offer them six books in a point-of-purchase display complete with signs you have professionally made at Kinko's. The store pays you only if they sell them and they don't have to return them if they don't sell; they may use them anyway they choose. They agree only to place them at their point of purchase (near the cash register) for 30 days. The advantages to them are that they get to try a new product at no risk. They do not have to go to the expense of returning or paying for what doesn't sell. You present the invoice with the conditions on it when you make your sales call.

This sales tool will be expensive only if you choose a retailer that is unsuited to your book. Even if some books end up not being paid for, they may be read or otherwise make their way into the community. You may have to give away fewer books this way than sending reader copies to retail outlets one at time and your results may be better in terms of sales.

Once you have a track record selling books as gifts, write up a marketing plan and present it to sales rep groups. You find them in "to the trade" buildings like The California Market Center in Los Angeles (www.californiamarketcenter.com) or the 225 Building, New York (www.225-fifth.com). Contact the building's offices, ask for a list of their showrooms, select ones that represent lines that fit with your book's subject matter and set up an appointment. Sell yourself first, then your book. Offer to do a signing at their next trade show or for accounts that buy a minimum number of books. You should know, that when retailers buy from sales reps, the sales are not returnable—a huge advantage to both publisher and author.

Attend gift trade shows and track down a like-minded representative there or advertise for a representative in a trade magazine like HOME DECOR BUYER (http://www.homedecorbuyer.com/) or GIFTS & DECORATIVE ACCESSORIES (www.giftsanddec.com).

> Caveat: Expect to pay a percentage of sales to representatives, usually ten to 15 percent of the wholesale price. Also expect that retailers will need 40 to 50 percent discount off the cover price. In order to do this discount, traditionally published authors may have to cut a deal with their publishers.

Chapter 37: Book Sales Getting Musty?

About Publishers, I conducted a study (employing my usual controls) that showed the average shelf life of a trade book to be somewhere between milk and yoghurt.

Calvin Trillin, US humorist

There is no way to keep a new book from going stale but if you keep reviving it, you might hold a classic in your hands.

Here are some suggestions for inexpensive battles you might wage with the preservation of your book in mind.

- The new magazine, SMALL PRESS REVIEW, is delivered to about six thousand bookstores—directly to the doors of book buyers and event planners. Edited by Ingrid Taylor (ding3433@sbcglobal.com), it includes informative articles useful for authors and small publishers. Go to http://www.smallpressreview.com to subscribe or to run an ad.
- Run a contest on your website or in your own newsletter. You can use your books for prizes but you might get some cross-promotion benefits if you ask other authors for books; many will give one to you in trade for the exposure. Watch the 99 cent stores for suitable favors to go with them.
- Barter your books for exposure in other authors' websites.
- Post your flyer, brochure, or business card on bulletin boards in grocery stores, coffee shops, Laundromats and bookstores.
- Offer classes in writing to your local high school, college or library system. Publicizing them costs little. The networking is invaluable. You can use this kind of experience in your media kit to show you have teaching and presentation skills.
- Slip auto-mailers that ask for recommendations into each book you sell or give out for publicity. It should include a

brief synopsis of your book, a picture of the cover of your book, your book's ISBN, ordering information, a couple of your most powerful blurbs, and a space for the reader to add her recommendation. Make it clear in the directions that the reader should fill out the form, address the envelope and mail it to a friend. Viral marketing is marketing like this that asks a customer to sell or suggest your product to others. It usually works best when a free gift is offered.

- Select your personal friends and readers from your mailing list, make labels and send them a note asking them to recommend your book to others or offer a perk like free shipping, gift wrap or small gift if they purchase your book for a friend.
- Though it may be a bit more expensive than some ideas in this book, learn more about Google's AdWords. Many authors of niche nonfiction or fiction that can be identified with strong keywords have found this advertising program extremely effective.
- While you're at the famous search engine, check out Google's AdSense for your own website. It is not easy to learn the intricacies of this advertising feature but if the fit is right, it may be advantageous to your marketing plan.
- Utilize lists:
  - Some of your reviews (both others' reviews of your book and reviews that you've written about others' books) have begun to age from disuse. Start posting them (with permission from the reviewer) on websites that allow you to do so.
  - Find leads on search engines, in the newsletters you've subscribed to or ask your fellow writers in e-groups about such sites. These change daily but an old tried and true one is www.review-books.com, Cheryl McCann, Editor.

> Note: This job should become an ongoing task. As your reviews proliferate so do links to your website (if you've added your URL to the author's information at the bottom of the review). With that kind of exposure comes requests like the one I received from a young journalist who writes for her college newspaper, The Indiana Daily Student. Her name is Cassidy Flanagan. She interviewed me when the doyenne of fashion publicity died because I once worked for her. She even

mentioned my books in her article, though they weren't essential to her subject.

- Record a playful message about your book on your answering machine.
- Judy Cummins is a book coach (judy@bookcoaching.com) who advises clients of the importance of headlines. So rewrite some snap into:
    - You article headlines and subheads.
    - Every feature in your e-zine. Every page and section on your website.
    - The subject lines in your outgoing e-mail.
    - Your advertising.
    - Your media releases.

Fight the urge to think it's too late. Don't be intimidated even when you see an article or newscast that didn't include you—but should have.

Getting lizard-spit green with envy is only useful if it prompts you to act. Call whoever was responsible for the coverage. Introduce yourself as someone who is available as a source next time. Be prepared to offer them a new slant, a new idea on a similar or different subject in which you can be an integral part of the story. Don't stop there. Add their e-mail address to your media-release list.

- Follow up with a letter outlining your ideas or expertise. Include a memento.
- Watch the vehicle where you saw this piece. When you see something by the same writer, send her a complimentary note.
- If you should land something big, follow up with your local press and TV assignment editors. Send them a release about your huge publicity coup.

Get in the promotion habit. At the grocery check-out stand, Janet Elaine Smith, a woman with a saucy sense of humor who wrote PAR FOR THE COURSE, offers the back of her book—complete with picture—instead of her driver's license. If the checker says there is no number on it she points to the ISBN. She has had clerks write it down. She says, "If they aren't convinced by the legality of this ploy, you still have an 'in' to tell them about your book." She then gives them a bookmark and autographs it so they won't throw it out. She is the brassiest of promoters but her books—none of them—have died inglorious deaths. All twelve of are available on www.amazon.com.

Get quoted. When you're editing your own work, notice the little nuggets floating around in your copy that are every bit as good as those quoted in Bartlett's. My mother was good at repeating homilies (she called these "tried and true sayings"). Oscar Wilde was a master at aphorisms. So is John Wooden, the legendary UCLA basketball coach and author, who must think them up at practices or at half time. "It's what you learn after you know it all that counts." was emblazoned across one of UCLA's extension division catalogs. The point is that being quoted is good branding. You'll note a few of my own and of others' quotes in this book. Several quote sites allow you to post your own zingers. NAWW (National Association of Women) will put a quote of the day in your mailbox if you sign up for it by sending a blank email to naww@onebox.com with "daily quote" in the subject window. You can use the same address to submit a quote of your own. This organization also published THE WOMAN'S BOOK OF POWERFUL QUOTATIONS (www.naww.org).

Plumb the Web again. The Web is the best tool of all for beginning promoters because it doesn't cost a single copper to learn what's effective and what's not and, if you goof or false-start, it isn't so damaging to your reputation. Here's a box full of ten FREE promotional gizmos that you can use effectively for your published book.

- Set up an autoresponder to send out samples of your book. Use a special e-mail address offered by some net providers or with an auto-service like www.sendfree.com. Post a provocative excerpt on it. Add the responder address to your e-mail signature. An autoresponder not only helps get a sample of your writing out to others easily and quickly, it's an aid in collecting the e-mails of those interested enough in your title to request that information! I always follow up with a personal note to those who requested information from my auto-responder (carolynhowardjohnson@sendfree.com).
- Link your page to like-minded sites as many times as possible. See how Annette Gisby uses links to her advantage on her "Silent Screams" site.

- Go to http://homepages.which.net/~LINKSA.htm; click on the "Free for All" links to see if what they offer will fit your branding image.
- Get your site listed on as many search engines possible. Go to www.ineedhits.com and www.addme.com. They'll lead you through a free-for-all listing spree at no cost.
- Go to www.yahoogroups.com. Choose a group of people who would be interested in your book. Choose another that shares promotion ideas. Jump into the fray. Ask questions and share your knowledge with fellow members of these groups. Your full contact information and a pitch should be included in your signature each time you post.

> Hint #1: As you read posts on your e-groups, pay attention to the signatures of others and where others are succeeding with their promotional efforts. Look for people and sites to review your book, interview you, publish your articles, and publish your next book.

> Hint #2: Visit sites that fit your goals. If they offer a newsletter, sign up to learn more. Keep contact names with e-mail addresses and notes about how they might be utilized in your promotion campaign. For a starter, go to www.SellWritingOnline.com.

Chapter 38: Success As a Motivator

The habit of celebrating helps me to acknowledge and enjoy the distance that I have already come along the writing path. By celebrating early and often, I appreciate more of the here-and-now.

Bruce Holland Rogers, from WORD WORKS

It's dangerous for your promotion efforts (and your writing) not to nod at your successes in the mirror. You may be prone to disparaging your own achievements. People who do that have trouble building confidence to try for more or better. Promotional successes kick-start a cycle only if we put them to use for us psychologically. Here's the formula:

```
Recognize a Success →Develop Confidence and
Promotion Skills → More Feelings of Success
```

Some Brits designed a site that business people use to help them with their presentations (www.presentationbiz.co.uk). They tell their visitors to "Visualise yourself succeeding." Short, sweet, and fine advice.

Sometimes we don't celebrate or visualize success because we don't recognize when we have achieved success. Was it that hard, black line that appears before us on a statement sent to us by a publisher last month? Will it be the appearance of our novel's name on The Times' Bestseller List? Was it the day we started commanding $2 a word as a freelancer? Or are these all mirages that are expunged by insecurity once we have achieved them?

This is a destructive cycle as old as Greek tragedy because it is part of our psychological make up. Nothing is ever enough. Success creeps up on us and then disappears because we are success myopic; we don't see it when it is sitting on the bridge of our noses. It's so easy to be infected by negativity; the news about everything from war to the state of publishing is just so dreadful.

The easiest way to recognize success is to write down goals. That way once we have met a goal, more recent expectations can't muss up our perspective. We'll know when we just won and can then celebrate.

What if the goal you jot down is to be just like Danielle Steele? Study her technique. Take classes. And then tap into your own originality. Many of us don't want to be the great D.S., but many do want to have their voices recognized as hers is. The chances are against us so when I feel less than successful, I reread WORD WORKS by Bruce Holland Rogers. It's perceptive, witty, perfectly written. Any of you ever heard of him? He has won several awards including the Nebula. He is a good example that even if you are big in all the ways that count, your name may not be a household word. So then, will we still not feel valued? Probably. Unless we learn a better way to recognize and view our successes.

Here's Your Horoscope for Successful Promoting:
Joyce Jillson advised this for one horoscope sign in May of 2004. It doesn't matter which sign because the advice is good for all writers any day of the year: "There are plenty of reasons to be proud. Write them down. If you don't celebrate the small wins, you don't have much to build on. It's all about momentum."

Appendix

Appendix I

SAMPLE MEDIA RELEASE: FOR AN EVENT

MEDIA RELEASE

Contact: Chuck Wikes,
Glendale Public Library Even Coordinator
Phone: mmmmmmm
Carolyn Howard-Johnson
Phone: mmmmmmmmmm
Fax: mmmmmmmmmmm
E-mail: HoJoNews@aol.com

For Release: March 5, 2003

Lecture Series Offers Three Faces of Tolerance

Glendale, CA—Three authors known for their stand against intolerance will be guests of the Friends of the Glendale Public Library Wednesday, March 5, at 7 p.m. at the library's central branch auditorium. The theme for the evening is "Three Faces of Tolerance."

Carolyn Howard-Johnson is the author of two award-winning, books, *This is the Place* and *Harkening: A Collection of Stories Remembered*. Both explore the corrosive nature of subtle intolerance. Dr. Alicia Ghiragossian is an internationally known poet who was nominated for the Nobel Prize. Of Armenian descent, she often writes of the Armenian Genocide. Stephen Veres' memoir, *A Light in the Distance*, tells his story of survival and triumph at the beginning of WWII in Budapest, Hungary.

Library Events Coordinator Chuck Wike is pleased that "these three exceptional local authors will discuss the intercultural challenges that face our community." Howard-Johnson and Ghirasgossian are residents of Glendale and Veres lives in Burbank. The event is cosponsored by the Glendale Human Relations Coalition.

Howard-Johnson's novel has won eight awards. Her book of nonfiction, *Harkening,* has won three. Her poetry and short stories appear frequently in literary journals and anthologies and she has appeared on TV and hundreds of radio stations nationwide. She also teaches classes for UCLA Extension's renowned Writers' Program.

Learn more at http://carolynhowardjohnson.com.

Full media kits, headshots, book cover art and more are available upon request both electronically and by post.

Appendix II

SAMPLE QUERY: FOR A FEATURE OR NEWS STORY

Note: The Follies features a cast of seniors so this letter targets that demographic. I chose this query as a sample so that you could see how to customize your own and so that you can see how to write a bio template (or paragraph) when your credentials are few. This query was among my very first. It was printed on a letterhead with complete contact information in the header and award logos in the footer.

The Follies Footlighter
Joelle Casteix, Editor
128 S. Palm Canyon Dr.
Palm Springs, CA. 92262

Dear Ms. Casteix:

What you at the Palm Springs Follies started is rather like a film of falling dominoes run in reverse—one domino after the other standing and marching into their older years with pride and gusto.

When I lived in Palm Springs and owned a business there (Carlan's Fine Gifts in the Palm Desert Mall), I attended your Follies many times. In fact it inspired me to begin a writing career at the age most are contemplating retirement. Then my successes encouraged my husband to begin a new life in acting. Your influence is indeed helping seniors like us stand erect.

In March, my first novel will be published. It was conceived in 1957, gestated for some 43 years and is about to be born.

It is going some place to have one's first novel published at 62 but I think that my story is typical of aging America and I know you agree. We are not getting older—we are rarifying.

Carolyn Howard-Johnson

If an old journalist like me reaches 50, she has a very good chance of making it to 90 in good health. She may have what was once a full lifetime ahead of her to do something else. Start a new career. Fight intolerance. Help raise a grandchild. You name it. I have done or am planning to do all of those things.

My first novel, THIS IS THE PLACE, is set in Utah at a time when that state is sure-enough in the news. The 2002 Winter Olympics. Polygamy. Bombings on Temple Square. There was even a cover story on genealogy in Time magazine last year. My love of genealogy was one of the inspirations for my book.

In February the Los Angeles Daily News ran a story on me and I have also been interviewed by a Los Angeles TV station. Most are finding that starting a new career at retirement the most interesting angle.

If you need more information you can find a picture (young-looking 62, no touch-ups!), a bio and the first two chapters of THIS IS THE PLACE by going to:
www.tlt.com/authors/carolynhowardjohnson.htm

I am enclosing a first person essay as well as a picture. I hope you can find room for me on the pages of your Follies Footlighter. If I can do anything else to help you, please let me know. Thank you so much for your time and consideration.

Sincerely,
Carolyn Howard-Johnson

Appendix III

SAMPLE QUERY: FOR AN INTERVIEW ON NATIONAL PUBLIC RADIO

Note: This letter got Christine Hohlbaum a gig on National Public Radio.
Notice the different thrust of this query from the one before this.
It focuses more on establishing expertise.

Dear Ashlee: **(Note the friendly opening, the name correctly spelled)**

Experts across the board agree that the first four years of a child's life are crucial. These crucial years are a time when the essential groundwork is laid for a child's future: language acquisition, social skills, and rapid brain development all take place during this time. **(Note that the author sets a professional tone, projects her expertise first thing.)**

Parents are often so busy juggling career and family that they find it challenging to give their children what they need. They feel isolated, discouraged, and helpless. **(Here is a suggested consequence if parents don't take advantage of the author's expertise.)**

How can they nurture their children while still maintaining their work lives? Despite how it may sometimes seem, children do not always need to be with their parents. In fact, they thrive even more when they are with a different number of trust-worthy people: day-care workers, relatives, family friends, etc. Exposure to many different settings can enhance a child's growth, not hinder it. **(Here she suggests benefits for those who access her expertise; both benefits and consequences will be important for NPR's own audience.)**

A playgroup is a great way for toddlers to first experience life outside of the home. It is fun, structured play with an educational element to it as well. I'd like to suggest a show about how to develop a toddler/preschooler playgroup as an easy guide for parents and child care workers to follow. **(Ahhh. A specific angle!)**

I have led numerous playgroups over the past few years in several languages. With over 140 published articles on parenting and child-rearing, I have the expertise to discuss parenting issues with authority and clarity. My debut collection of short stories, Diary of a Mother: Parenting Stories and Other Stuff, has also been well-received by an astounding breadth of readers. **(Here the author establishes her expertise with concrete credentials.)**

I look forward to hearing with you about my show suggestion, "How to Develop a Toddlers' Playgroup in Five Easy Steps". I will be in Virginia at the end of May for six weeks in the event that you like your guests to appear at the station. Please see the attached article for your convenience.**(And here, Hohlbaum takes care of business— everything that Ashlee needs to make an interview a reality.)**

Warm regards, **(Hohlbaum's close is not overly formal or overly familiar.)**
Christine Louise Hohlbaum

Christine Louise Hohlbaum, American author of DIARY OF A MOTHER: PARENTING STORIES AND OTHER STUFF lives near Munich, Germany, with her husband and two children. Hohlbaum offers a class on book promotion at http://www.momsinprint.com/christine.html.When she is not writing, teaching, leading toddler playgroups or wiping up messes, she generally prefers to frolic in the Bavarian countryside. Visit her web site at: http://www.DiaryofaMother.com.

Appendix IV
SAMPLE FORM: FOR BUILDING YOUR READER LIST

Jane WhataWriter, Author of SUNRISE
EVENT FORM
(Information you provide me remains with me. I use it to
better serve my audience.)

>PLEASE PRINT<

Name of This Event:

_____   City:

_____Date: _____

Your Name

| | | | | | | | | | | | | | | | | | | | | | | | | | | | |

Address

| | | | | | | | | | | | | | | | | | | | | | | | | | | | | | | |

City |__|__|__|__|__|__|__|__|__|__|__|__| State_____ Zip____

E-mail

_____

Are you now on my mailing list? (Please circle one.) Y   N
How many of my events have you attended? _____

Would you like me to inform you of my future appearances
or events? Y   N   Future Books? Y   N

Please comment on today's event so I can do a better job for
you next time. Assign a rating from 1 (worst) to 10:

   Overall rating of the event: _____ Food and/or snacks:
_____
   The readings I selected: _____ My reading
ability:_____
   Facilities: _____
   Did I excite your interest in my writings?_____
   My handouts: _____
   Day of week and time of event selected:_____

My helpers: _____   Acoustics:

_____

Please give me suggestions for improving my next event:

Would you like to be one of my volunteer helpers at my next event? Y   N

Please give me information about someone you know who might want to attend my next event.
Name
|__|__|__|__|__|__|__|__|__|__|__|__|__|__|__|__|__|__|__|__|__|__|__|__|__|__|__|__|__|

Address
|__|__|__|__|__|__|__|__|__|__|__|__|__|__|__|__|__|__|__|__|__|__|__|__|__|__|__|__|__|

City |__|__|__|__|__|__|__|__|__|__|__|__|__| State_____
Zip_____

Do you know of an organization that might be interested in having me as a speaker?

Any final comments?

Index

Books by Carolyn Howard-Johnson

THIS IS THE PLACE,
an award-winning novel

ISBN 1588513521

HARKENING: A COLLECTION OF STORIES REMEMBERED,
a book of award winning creative nonfiction

ISBN 1591295505

Contact the author at HoJoNews@aol.com or visit her websites, http://carolynhowardjohnson.com or www.authorsden.com/carolynhowardjohnson.

About the Author

Carolyn Howard-Johnson was a fashion publicist for a prominent New York City agency and an editorial assistant for GOOD HOUSEKEEPING MAGAZINE. She has also been a columnist for THE SALT LAKE TRIBUNE and THE PASADENA STAR NEWS. She used her promotion skills when her first novel, THIS IS THE PLACE was published. It has won eight awards including one for sales and marketing from her publisher. Her second book, HARKENING: A COLLECTION OF STORIES REMEMBERED, is a winner of three awards.

Howard-Johnson's fiction, nonfiction and poems have appeared in national magazines, anthologies and review journals. She speaks on culture, tolerance and other subjects and has appeared on TV and hundreds of radio stations nationwide. She is an instructor for UCLA Extension's Writers' Program. She loves to travel and has studied writing at Cambridge University in the United Kingdom; Herzen University in St. Petersburg, Russia; and Charles University in Prague as well as the University of Southern California and UCLA.

Films and books are her passions and she reviews them on several websites and in print. She admits to loving public relations almost as much as writing.

Printed in the United States
152521LV00003BA/18/A